secrets

A Guide to Simplifying the Art of
Heart Healthy and Diabetic Cooking

of HEALTHY COOKING

by Barbara Seelig-Brown

American
Diabetes
Association.

Director, Book Publishing, Abe Ogden; Managing Editor, Greg Guthrie; Acquisitions Editor, Rebekah Renshaw; Editor, Rebekah Renshaw; Production Manager, Melissa Sprott; Composition, pixiedesign, llc; Cover Design, Jenn French; Photographer, Renee Comet; Printer, Versa Press.

Printed in the United States of America
1 3 5 7 9 10 8 6 4 2

The suggestions and information contained in this publication are generally consistent with the *Standards of Medical Care in Diabetes* and other policies of the American Diabetes Association, but they do not represent the policy or position of the Association or any of its boards or committees. Reasonable steps have been taken to ensure the accuracy of the information presented. However, the American Diabetes Association cannot ensure the safety or efficacy of any product or service described in this publication. Individuals are advised to consult a physician or other appropriate health care professional before undertaking any diet or exercise program or taking any medication referred to in this publication. Professionals must use and apply their own professional judgment, experience, and training and should not rely solely on the information contained in this publication before prescribing any diet, exercise, or medication. The American Diabetes Association—its officers, directors, employees, volunteers, and members—assumes no responsibility or liability for personal or other injury, loss, or damage that may result from the suggestions or information in this publication.

♾ The paper in this publication meets the requirements of the ANSI Standard Z39.48-1992 (permanence of paper).

ADA titles may be purchased for business or promotional use or for special sales. To purchase more than 50 copies of this book at a discount, or for custom editions of this book with your logo, contact the American Diabetes Association at the address below, at booksales@diabetes.org, or by calling 703-299-2046.

American Diabetes Association
1701 North Beauregard Street
Alexandria, Virginia 22311

DOI: 10.2337/9781580405447

Library of Congress Cataloging-in-Publication Data

Seelig-Brown, Barbara.
  Secrets of healthy cooking / Barbara Seelig-Brown.
    pages cm
  Includes bibliographical references and index.
  ISBN 978-1-58040-544-7 (alk. paper)
  1. Cooking. I. Title.
  TX714.S44 2015
  641.5--dc23
                        2015002619

for dad
SOME GIRLS JUST GET LUCKY!

acknowledgments

Thank you to Rebekah Renshaw for considering this idea and making it such a fun project. Thank you for fine tuning the idea, the content, the recipes, and the photos as we went along. It is always a joy to work with you. Thank you to Abe Ogden for trusting Rebekah and I with this idea. Your insight is invaluable. Thank you to all at the American Diabetes Association who helped in any way, even though I might not have known it.

Thank you to Renee Comet, Lisa Cherkasky, Carolyn Schimley, Steven Redfearn, and Audrey Kenney for the beautiful recipe photos. I always love seeing your finished products!

Thank you to Cathy Miller for the *how to* photos that appear throughout the book and for your patience during the process. I love when you are feelin' it!

Thank you to all my friends and family who served as recipe testers and tasters. Your comments and friendship made this so much fun.

Thank you to my family at 45 Ocean for the support I have received from you while creating this book as well as a new life.

Thank you Barone for the privilege of doing what I love.

Food is love: and this book, as all of my cooking, is about the love of family and friends. Thank you all. BUON APPETITO!

—Barb

table
of CONTENTS

part 1
THE BASICS

building a pantry for healthy cooking

One of the keys to a stress free cooking experience is to keep your house well stocked so you can spend less time in the grocery store and more time cooking. I would rather be home in my bunny slippers, listening to my favorite music, and sipping wine while preparing dinner for my family than standing in a takeout or grocery store line. Use this list as your pantry-stocking list and then just add the fresh items from the perimeter of the store as necessary.

Pantry

- Extra virgin olive oil
- Canola oil
- Balsamic, white balsamic, and wine vinegars
- Sea salt—fine grind
- Garlic—fresh, whole heads
- Onions
- Shallots
- Peppercorns and a good-quality pepper mill
- All-purpose flour
- Yeast
- Light brown sugar
- Honey
- Granulated sugar
- Pasta—a variety of shapes and sizes
- Rice—jasmine, arborio
- Beans—canned black beans, pink beans, chickpeas, and small white
- Lentils—de Puy, brown, and red
- Polenta/corn meal
- Evaporated skim milk
- Canned broth and stock—chicken, beef, mushroom, and vegetable
- Canned diced tomatoes, crushed tomatoes, and tomato paste
- Chunk white tuna in spring water
- Anchovies—rolled fillets with capers
- Clams
- Fruits—canned such as mandarin oranges, apricots, and crushed pineapple
- Fruits—dried fruits such as raisins, cherries, and apricots

Refrigerator

- Low-fat cottage cheese
- Part-skim ricotta

- Crumbled gorgonzola—low-fat, if available
- Low-fat plain yogurt
- Light cream cheese bricks—also labeled Neufchatel, 1/3 less fat
- Fresh mozzarella
- Parmigiano-Reggiano cheese
- Eggs—large
- Mustard—variety
- Capers
- Vermouth—dry white
- Wine—dry white
- Lemons, limes, oranges
- Salad greens—a variety of types, textures, and colors
- Fresh baby spinach and/or kale
- Carrots
- Celery
- Fresh herbs—basil, oregano, rosemary
- Sun-dried tomatoes—not in oil
- Olives

Freezer

- Filled pastas—such as tortellini and agnolotti
- Homemade breadcrumbs
- Artichokes
- Baby corn
- Peas
- String beans—whole
- Pearl onions
- Ground beef and/or buffalo meat
- Turkey cuts—such as ground, breast, sausage
- Chicken breast—boneless and skinless, individually wrapped
- Roasting chickens—5-6 pounds, washed and then frozen
- Large shrimp—cooked, peeled, and deveined
- Large shrimp—uncooked, peeled, and deveined
- Individually frozen fish fillets—such as whiting or halibut
- Individually frozen center-cut pork chops
- Blueberries, raspberries, strawberries
- Pignoli nuts
- Crepes

Additional Items

- Anything you love to cook with!

By keeping these items on hand, you will be able to come home from a busy day and put together a colorful, delicious meal in no time using the recipes found in any of my cookbooks.

general secrets and tips for a healthy kitchen

- Read recipes thoroughly before beginning to cook.

- Make sure you understand all of the ingredients and cooking terms.

- Prepare what is referred to as *mise en place*. It means that you gather all the ingredients, do all the prep such as washing, measuring, slicing, and dicing, and have everything ready before turning on the stove, mixer, or food processor.

- When preparing yeast bread use your meat thermometer to make sure that the water or milk is at the proper temperature, which is between 110–120 degrees.

- Your oven is a perfect rising place. Leave the oven turned off but turn the oven light on. It is warm and draft free.

- Drain and rinse anything from a can. You will remove as much of any potential preservatives or flavorings that could influence your dish.

- Draining canned beans helps to remove any preservatives and some of the gas.

- Purchase the highest-quality cheeses that you can for more flavor. You will be able to use less and save calories.

- Stock your kitchen with helpful tools (See Essential Equipment List, page 7).

- Use a grater/zester for grating cheese, garlic, nutmeg, and chocolate, and for zesting citrus.

- Use a flat meat pounder for pounding meat or chopping nuts in plastic bags.

- Toast nuts by placing them in a small dry skillet and cooking until golden. Remove from pan and cool. Place in plastic bag and roughly chop with your meat pounder.

- If your oven has a convection setting, use it to save time. Convection ovens generally cook food in 25% less time, so make sure to figure that in before setting your oven timer. Since convection ovens have a fan that evenly circulates heat, you will have more even browning as well.

- Keep extra stock or broth on hand. This will help you in a pinch if a pan needs to be deglazed, a soup needs a little more flavor or liquid, or a sauce needs a boost. Purchase stock in large quantities and store for use all week. It will keep up to 10 days once opened.

- Use jams or all-fruit, no-sugar fruit spreads for glazing cakes, finishing tarts, etc.

- Crush and peel garlic quickly with a chef's knife using this method: Place one clove of garlic on a cutting board. Place the flat side of a chef's knife on top of the garlic. With your other hand, give the chef's knife a good strong whack over the garlic. Lift up the knife and remove the papery garlic skin. The garlic is also partially chopped. Continue chopping with a rocking motion until you have desired size.

- SALAD TIPS: Salad should not be swimming in dressing. It's better to add less and decide you need more. Drying your greens in a salad spinner will help dressing cling to the greens rather than sinking to the bottom of the salad bowl. Slowly whisking in the oil allows for a better emulsion.

- The drier your greens are when storing them, the longer they will last. Wash them, spin them dry, lay them on paper towels, roll up, and place in a plastic bag.

- SIGNATURE HERB BLEND: Go through your herbs and spices and create your own "signature blend" that will be a shortcut way to season anything you are cooking. For instance, if you frequently use basil, parsley, and rosemary, go ahead and pre-mix them, add salt and pepper if desired, and you have your own signature herb blend ready to use. Or prepare my Stress Free Cooking Seasoning Blends on page 9.

- Wondra is a great addition to the pantry. It is granulated flour that makes smooth sauces and also is good for searing and sautéing as it is finer and lighter than all-purpose flour and will absorb less oil.

- Place leftover artisan or homemade breads in your food processor to create your own breadcrumbs and freeze them.

- Plan meals ahead of time so that you can properly defrost ingredients and know that you have everything on hand.

- Remember to cook pasta in at least 4–6 quarts of water. Cooking pasta in too small a pot or too little water will result in sticky, gummy pasta. Use a larger pot than you think you will need.

- Easy asparagus trimming: Just hold it in both hands and bend. The ends will naturally break off at the correct place.

- Keep your knives sharp (this will make your work go much quicker). A sharp knife is actually safer than a dull one.

- Use a larger bowl or pan than you think you will need so that you don't have to switch during the cooking process.

- Make enough salad dressing to last several days.

- Use a crockpot to cook soups, stews, and sauces while you are out.

- If the recipe calls for fresh herbs and you have only dried, you can convert dry to fresh with this ratio: 1 part dry = 3 parts fresh.

- Edible flowers include nasturtiums, pansies, roses, marigolds, hibiscus, and herb flowers. They are great garnishes and additions to salads.

- Deglazing is a technique that lifts the browned bits from the bottom of the pan after sautéing, browning, or searing. Simply add some liquid such as wine, stock, or water to the hot pan and the bits will be released, creating a more flavorful sauce.

- A vegetable steamer is handy but if you don't have one, simply place the veggies in a pan with a tight fitting lid, add an inch or two of water, and cook 5–10 minutes until tender. Make sure you don't let the water evaporate completely, so watch the pan closely.

- To butterfly a piece of meat such as a pork tenderloin or boneless turkey breast, place the meat on the flat work surface. Find the horizontal center and cut one-third of the way into the meat so that you can unfold it to one side. Repeat with other side and open the meat so that it is flat.

- Keep a permanent magic marker in your kitchen so that you can date containers as soon as you open them and you won't throw out as much "questionable" food.

- When I have leftover cheeses that I think might not keep well, I place them in my food processor and shred them and then freeze them for future cooking.

essential equipment list

- Dough or bench scraper—to scrape pizza dough from counter
- Egg slicer for slicing eggs, olives, and strawberries
- Kitchen twine
- Flat meat pounder—This tool does not pierce the meat. An even thickness of meat allows for more even cooking.
- Food processor—for shredding cheese, slicing veggies, or making dough
- Graduated sets of mixing bowls in glass or stainless steel—Always use a larger bowl than you think you will need so that you don't have to switch to a larger bowl once you have begun cooking.
- Grater/zester—for finely zested citrus, or finely grating cheese
- Half sheet pans for baking and roasting veggies
- Immersion blender—for quick pureeing right in the pot
- Instant-read meat thermometer—Never overcook anything again and always get the right water temperature for recipes that use yeast.
- Knives: chef's knife, paring knife, slicing knife, and serrated knife for soft foods such as bread and tomatoes

- PANS:

  8-, 10-, 12-inch sauté or fry pans, both nonstick and traditional finish

  Sauteuse Pan—looks like a sauté pan but has two loop handles and goes conveniently into the oven

  Grill pan

  3- and 4-quart saucepans

  8-quart stock or soup pot
- Parchment paper—alleviates need for additional fat in pan and makes cleanup easier
- Pizza stone
- Pizza cutter/wheel
- Salad spinner—Greens last longer when stored with less water.
- Stand mixer
- Tongs—they do not pierce meat when turning, also great for tossing salad
- Vertical chicken roaster—I love the Spanek Vertical Roaster. It alleviates the need for fat in the pan and any fat completely drains away from the bird.

herb and spice guide

The Most Commonly Used Herbs and Seasonings in This Book

- BASIL—A favorite in Italian cooking and a favorite of mine. There are many varieties of basil, most of which are green but occasionally you will see purple varieties. It is the main ingredient in pesto but also complements tomatoes and cheese especially well. The flavor can vary from fresh and pungent to almost licorice-like. It is a member of the mint family.

- ITALIAN OR FLAT PARSLEY—There is also a curly parsley but I prefer to use the Italian or flat leaf variety as it is more flavorful. The stems are edible and contain a lot of flavor. Parsley keeps well in the fridge for several days if stored with as little water as possible. A salad spinner is a great way to wash and "dry" your parsley, lettuce, and other herbs. The curly variety was originally used as a breath freshener in Victorian times.

- ROSEMARY—Rosemary is also a member of the mint family. It is a Mediterranean herb and thrives in dry climate. Rosemary is delicious with lamb, chicken, and roasted potatoes. If you have large stems of rosemary, the woody stems also make great skewers for hors d'oeuvres.

- GARLIC—The garlic as a whole is referred to as a bulb, the individual pieces are cloves. Garlic is pungent when raw and mellows as it is cooked. It is delicious sautéed and roasted. Garlic is a member of the Allium family and has been thought to have medicinal purposes and also to ward off evil spirits.

- FINE SEA SALT—There are several salt choices. The most common are sea salt, kosher salt, and table salt. Sea salt is the least processed and contains no additives. Table salt has additives to retain its white color and keep it free flowing.

- STRESS FREE COOKING SEASONING BLEND—Having this blend on hand will be a time saver for you. Use this for all your cooking. See recipe on page 9.

- STRESS FREE COOKING ITALIAN SEASONING BLEND—Also a time saver, when you are feeling "Italian," make this your go-to seasoning. See recipe on page 9.

- BLACK PEPPER—One of the most widely used spices in the world, it has a spicy flavor and mixes well with salt.

- CRUSHED RED PEPPER—This consists of dried and crushed chili peppers. It adds a lot of spicy heat to dishes and is a favorite on pizza and pasta dishes.

How to Grow Your Own Herb Garden

Some herbs are very delicate and can be difficult to grown in your kitchen but you can always try them in your sunniest window. Most herbs like to dry out in between watering. If the climate is hot and sunny they will thrive outside as opposed to inside.

If a recipe calls for fresh herbs and you only have dry on hand, you an easily convert to dry and vice versa. The ratio of fresh to dry is 3 to 1, so you will use 3 times the amount of fresh to dry. Remember that when fresh herbs are lighter and fluffier and when they are dried, they lose the water and therefore are "smaller."

How to Make Your Own Spice Blends

In this book, I have created some spice blends as a shortcut for you. They are the Stress Free Cooking Seasoning Blend and Stress Free Cooking Italian Seasoning Blend, found below. You can also create your own spice blend by combining some of your favorite and most commonly used spices together just as I have done with my blends.

stress free cooking seasoning blend

SERVES: 15 | SERVING SIZE: 1 TEASPOON

1 tablespoon onion powder

1 tablespoon garlic powder

1 tablespoon Italian seasoning blend

1 tablespoon celery seed

1 tablespoon fine sea salt

1 tablespoon freshly milled black pepper

1 | Mix all ingredients and store in an airtight container at room temperature.

EXCHANGES/CHOICES Free Food | **CALORIES** 5 | **CALORIES FROM FAT** 0
TOTAL FAT 0.0 g | **SATURATED FAT** 0.0 g | **TRANS FAT** 0.0 g
CHOLESTEROL 0 mg | **SODIUM** 435 mg | **POTASSIUM** 25 mg
TOTAL CARBOHYDRATE 1 g | **DIETARY FIBER** 0 g | **SUGARS** 0 g
PROTEIN 0 g | **PHOSPHORUS** 5 mg

stress free cooking italian seasoning blend

SERVES: 18 | SERVING SIZE: 1 TEASPOON

1 tablespoon onion powder

1 tablespoon garlic powder

1 tablespoon celery seed

1 tablespoon fine sea salt

1 tablespoon freshly milled black pepper

1 teaspoon dried oregano

1 teaspoon dried rosemary

1 teaspoon dried parsley

1 | Mix all ingredients and store in an airtight container at room temperature.

EXCHANGES/CHOICES Free Food | **CALORIES** 5 | **CALORIES FROM FAT** 0
TOTAL FAT 0.0 g | **SATURATED FAT** 0.0 g | **TRANS FAT** 0.0 g
CHOLESTEROL 0 mg | **SODIUM** 365 mg | **POTASSIUM** 20 mg
TOTAL CARBOHYDRATE 1 g | **DIETARY FIBER** 0 g | **SUGARS** 0 g
PROTEIN 0 g | **PHOSPHORUS** 5 mg

freezing 101

Food preparation can be much simpler when you have high-quality, extremely fresh ingredients. Finding the time to prepare food is probably more of an issue than the effort it takes to preserve foods for the future or as a do-ahead plan. However, freezing does not take as much time as canning, which makes it more do-able for busy families. Spending a few hours chopping and freezing is time well spent, especially when you are savoring the fruits (or veggies) of your labor in mid January and February. Be advised that vegetables with high water content such as mushrooms, cucumbers, celery, onions, and lettuce do not freeze well.

I always keep a roll of freezer tape and a permanent magic marker in my kitchen along with a supply of plastic bags, foil pans, and plastic containers. Labeling is key to freezing. If you keep food for a few weeks or months in your freezer, it is very possible and probably likely that you won't remember what it is after a while. I include the name of the food, the date I froze it, and also cooking time and temp if it is possible that I will be sharing this item with someone.

Basil or Fresh Herb Paste

Place fresh herbs in your food processor and pulse to finely mince. Slowly add extra virgin olive oil, approximately 1 tablespoon at a time, until a "paste" consistency is achieved. This mixture can be placed in small snack-size plastic bags containing 1–2 tablespoons each. Place the small bags inside a larger one for easier storage and freeze. When you are cooking and need fresh herbs, you can reach into your freezer for some herb paste, which will add a very fresh taste to any salad dressing, soup, stew, or sauce. There is an added time-saving benefit in that some of the work has already been done for you, eliminating the need to chop herbs each time you prepare a meal. You can also make blends of your favorite herbs and include garlic if you wish.

Tomatoes

Tomatoes can be chopped and frozen for future cooking or made into a puree and frozen or canned. Fresh, frozen, chopped tomatoes are quick and easy to freeze and use later in sauces. If you want to make sauce before freezing, keep it simple so that it is more versatile when needed. I generally boil my tomatoes for 2–3 minutes, just enough to blister the skins and make them easy to remove. Once the tomatoes are boiled, you plunge them into cold water and the skins will come right off. Peel the tomatoes, and place in a large pot, add your fresh basil and sautéed garlic and cook for several hours to reduce the water content. Freeze in quantities that are appropriate for your household.

Corn

Fresh ears of corn can be blanched in boiling water for 2–3 minutes, cooled, then placed in freezer bags. Corn can also be blanched and cut from the cob and frozen.

Peppers

Peppers can be cut into desired shapes and sizes and frozen. When defrosted they will be slightly limp, due to their high water content, but they will be good for cooking.

Zucchini/Yellow Squash

Zucchini and other squashes can be *lightly* sautéed in extra virgin olive oil and frozen.

Fruits
(such as peaches, strawberries, and blueberries)

Fruits can be peeled, cut, and placed in freezer bags or containers for use during the winter. You can use them in ice creams, sorbets, muffins, pies, cobblers, or fruit sauces.

fish know-how

We all know that we should incorporate more fish into our diet. It is low in fat, high in protein, and contains valuable vitamins and minerals, as well as omega-3 oils, which are polyunsaturated. The type of fat we consume is relevant for a heart-healthy diet, that being less than 30% of all calories from fat with less than 10% coming from saturated fats. Studies have been done showing that a healthy diet featuring a variety of foods, including fish, can actually decrease the risk for coronary disease and certain cancers, as well as increase longevity. Since people with diabetes are also at risk for heart disease, fish is an important component.

Many people shy away from cooking fish because they just don't know how to buy, store, or cook it. Let's start with some basics so that we can keep it simple. Dinner at home should be enjoyable, and some fish basics will make that possible. Keep it simple and fresh. One of the best things about fish is that you don't need to do a lot to it. In fact, you don't want to overpower it. Of course, if you don't like fish, then disguising it with strong flavors is for you.

Shopping and Storage

Fish should smell sweet or smell like the ocean. Smelly fish is old and not for you. When you look at the fish counter, it should look appetizing and fresh. The fish you see should be shiny, firm, and if whole, the eyes should be clear. Many supermarkets do not even carry whole fish because the demand for them is not as great as more common varieties like shellfish and fillets. Whole fish is generally available at a good fish store and is worth the effort to find it.

Just like meat, fish on the bone is more tender and succulent. When you are shopping, you should buy your fish last and ask for it to be put on ice so that you don't have to worry about food safety. When you arrive home, put it away first. You can store it either wrapped in waxed paper, in a tightly sealed plastic container, or on top of a bed of ice placed in a colander in a bowl. Use fresh fish within a day of purchasing. Always check with the fish manager as to when the fish was delivered to the store. A good fish manager will tell you when it comes in and will also tell you what the best value is on the day you are shopping. I always give the experts their due and rely on them to help me get just what I need.

Cooking and Testing for Doneness

A general rule of thumb for cooking fish is 10 minutes per inch of thickness. A one-inch thick fillet should take at least 10 minutes to cook. Another way to check is to see if it flakes when pierced with a fork; however, for some varieties, such as salmon and tuna, this would be considered overcooked. A meat thermometer is your best friend. To retain flavor, tuna, salmon, and swordfish should be cooked to an internal temperature of 125°F. Fish steaks, fillets, or whole fish should be cooked to an internal temperature of 140°F. White-flesh fish should look opaque when cooked. Clams, mussels, and oysters are cooked until their shells open. Discard any that do not open. Shellfish like shrimp and lobster are cooked until pink and opaque.

The Recipes

The recipes in this book were developed with the thought that you could interchange the cooking methods, sauces, marinades, and side dishes.

Types of Fish

There are endless varieties of fish to choose from. Depending on what part of the country you live in and also what season we are in, certain species will or will not be available. You can purchase some of the harder-to-find varieties of fish and seafood directly from the fishermen through the Internet.

The most commonly eaten fish are salmon and tuna. There are many recipes using these varieties. You should decide what your feelings are on wild vs. farm-raised, along with the varieties that are surrounded by the mercury controversy, such as tuna and swordfish. Yes, wild salmon is more nutritious than farm-raised, but if it is not available or the cost is prohibitive, farm-raised will do. There are also social responsibilities to consider. Do you feel right knowing that a specific variety might become extinct because it is overfished? I choose not to overeat these varieties, but I know

many people who feel that if it is in the stores, you should buy it. Remember one thing, research is constantly changing and nutrition is constantly being re-evaluated.

Methyl mercury is a substance in our environment; the main sources of toxic mercury are from power plants that burn fossil fuels and coal. Mercury accumulates in streams, oceans, rivers, and lakes. After a chemical transformation, it becomes toxic. Fish absorb the mercury by feeding on aquatic organisms. Mercury is more prominent in larger fish, as they survive by eating the smaller ones. Older fish also contain more mercury than younger ones, because they are exposed longer. Of course, we can't really tell how old a fish is, so we need to exercise our own good judgment.

Vulnerable and sensitive populations, such as young children, pregnant women, women of childbearing age who might become pregnant, or nursing mothers should avoid excessive consumption of high-mercury fish. The most widely accepted recommendation for women of childbearing age is 8 ounces of uncooked fish or 6 ounces of cooked fish per week and 3 ounces of uncooked and 2 ounces of cooked fish for children. There are differing opinions on just how much fish containing higher levels of mercury should be consumed by anyone. For more information, consult FDA data, Mercury Levels in Seafood Species, or the EPA, which is endorsed by the National Academy of Sciences.

choosing meat and poultry

When choosing any item in the grocery store you should always look for the freshest, most attractive product. Color is important. Red meat should be red, not brown. It should also be firm and slightly moist. Look for cuts that have the least amount of visible fat. Pork should be grayish pink and chicken should look creamy white to deep yellow, with few juices in the package.

Always check the sell-by dates. If there are several packages on display, look at several to make sure you are getting a product with the longest shelf life. I never buy the package of meat that is $1 or $2 off because today is the last sell-by date. Never choose packages that are torn or are leaking.

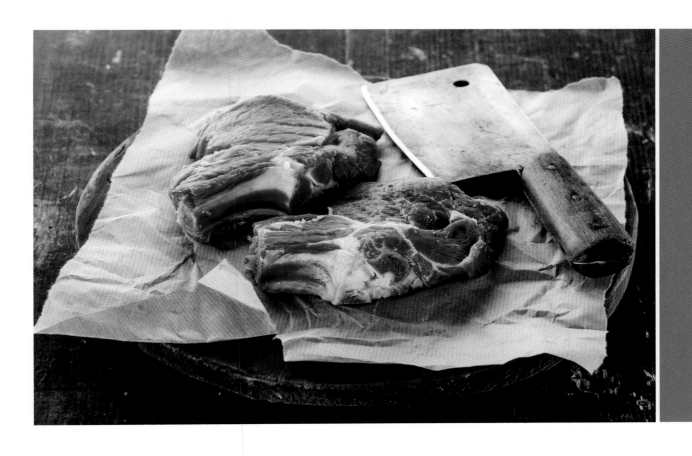

kitchen glossary

Most Common Cooking Terms

AL DENTE—in Italian this means "to the tooth" because pasta should not be overcooked. It should have a little bite and give slight resistance when eaten.

BASTE—to keep foods moist during cooking by spooning liquid over the food.

BLANCH—to partially cook fruits or vegetables for use in recipes that require further cooking or before freezing.

BRAISE—to cook foods in small amounts of liquid for long periods of time. Foods should be covered while cooking. Commonly used for less tender cuts of meat.

BROWN—to cook food in a skillet or sauté pan until golden brown on each side, usually in a small amount of extra virgin olive oil or canola oil.

CHOP—to cut foods in small pieces. *Also known as:* mince—a smaller cut than chop and dice. A proper dice is 1/4–1/8 inch in size.

CRUSH—An example would be to crush and peel a clove of garlic. Place one clove garlic on cutting board. Place the flat side of a chef's knife on top of the garlic. With your other hand, give the chef's knife a good strong whack over the garlic. Lift up the knife and remove the papery garlic skin.

CHIFFONADE—a form of chopping. Commonly used with basil, you stack several basil leaves on top of one another and roll them up. Using a chef's knife you slice the roll into long thin strips. The strips are then unrolled and used in the recipe.

DEGLAZE—adding water, wine, or stock to the pan after browning so that you can easily remove the fond (browned bits) from the pan. This is the basis for a full-flavored sauce.

FOLD—gently mix ingredients. Use a rubber spatula and cut down vertically through the mixture from the back of the bowl. Repeat until well blended.

FOND—the browned bits that remain in the pan after browning meat.

GARNISH—to add a finishing touch, usually an herb in the dish.

GRATE—to rub food across a grating surface to make very fine pieces or shreds.

JULIENNE—to cut into long thin strips, similar to a matchstick.

KNEAD—to work dough, incorporating air, until it is smooth and elastic. This can be done in a food processor, quality stand mixer, or with the heel of your hand.

MARINADE—to soak food in a mixture of flavorful liquid ingredients. A basic vinaigrette can be used for an all-purpose marinade. Meat can be marinated for indefinite periods, even several days, but fish generally only 20 minutes, and chicken for several hours.

POACH—to cook food by submerging it in liquid just below the boil. See the recipe for Poaching Chicken on page 73.

PUREE—to process or mash food until it is as smooth as possible, generally in a food processor, a stick blender, or food mill.

REDUCE—to decrease the volume of liquid in a pan by a certain amount. As the liquid evaporates flavor intensifies and some liquids will thicken.

SIMMER—cooking food just below the boiling point.

STEAM—to cook in steam given off by minimal liquid. The food is generally in a basket above the liquid.

how to read a recipe

Are you sometimes confused or intimidated by the way a recipe is written? Do things come out differently than you expected? As a professional recipe developer I follow certain guidelines—the gold standards, if you will—for writing recipes. My goal is to make my recipes as clear as possible so that you will enjoy cooking at home and do it more often.

One very important point that I like to bring up to my readers and students is that there are many variables in a recipe. Variables can be things like interpretation, pan size, type of pan, type of stove, ingredient quality, atmosphere, and so much more. If a recipe does not turn out perfectly, it is not necessarily your fault. It could be the result of one of the variables. Since our stoves, equipment, and ingredient quality can vary greatly, recipes should include descriptors such as: cook chicken breast 3 minutes on each side or until golden brown on each side. Perhaps the recipe developer had a gas stove and yours is electric. The timing will vary greatly but the end result can still be similar by noting the descriptor—golden brown. Is the quality of the recipe developer's pan and your pan identical? It is highly unlikely that we all have the same supplies or equipment in our kitchens.

Ingredients should be listed in the order in which they are added in the preparation or cooking method.

Mise en place is your best friend! This means that you read the recipe thoroughly and perform all necessary prep before turning on the stove, mixer, or food processor. If the recipe prep calls for pounded chicken or sliced mushrooms, do it as part of the *mise en place*. Measure the stock, peel the garlic, chop the onions, and zest the lemon. Does the recipe call for ingredients at room temperature? This can take 20–30 minutes once removed from the refrigerator. Does something need to be defrosted? *Mise en place* will help guide you through the cooking process. For instance, sautéing garlic takes only minutes but pounding the chicken breast can take much longer. The pounding should be done before the garlic hits the pan, to avoid scorching the garlic.

User Guidelines for Reading Recipes

- Always read a recipe in its entirety before starting the cooking process
- Be sure that you have all ingredients on hand
- Be sure that you understand all the techniques and terms in the recipe
- Prepare ingredients *mise en place*
- Look for descriptors
- Trust your judgment
- Don't be intimidated
- Have fun

basic wine pairing

Many wine experts today will acknowledge that you should drink what you like with the food that you like. While this may sound oversimplified, it speaks to the fact that there is so much out there to choose from, why not? Perhaps your taste leans towards spicy food. It is likely that you will also lean toward a fuller wine with more spice.

The basics of pairing food and wine should be considered when selecting a wine for a meal but should not paralyze or restrict you.

- Don't let one overwhelm the other.

- Think about the ingredients in the dish, not just the main ingredient such as fish, chicken, etc. Is there acidity, sweetness, or spice? The wine should be paired with the boldest flavor.

- If there is acidity in both the food and wine, the acidity will recede and the other characteristics will come out.

- If there is earth in wine, there should be less in the food or the flavor will be overwhelmingly earthy.

- Glass shape will help to reveal the wine's best characteristics. For instance, a white wine glass is smaller and more tapered at the top to keep the chill on the wine, a red wine glass more open to allow the wine to breathe, and a champagne glass is tall and narrow to allow the bubbles to flourish.

One of my personal favorite guidelines for pairing is to keep the wines local, that is, Italian wine with Italian dishes or Portuguese wine with Portuguese food. I also pair by thinking in this manner: casual wine with casual food, champagne with hors d'oeuvres and special occasion foods; although Italian prosecco and French champagne seem to go with just about anything!

There are many philosophies on food and wine pairing. You must find and adopt or develop one that works for you. The general feeling today is that wine should not be a mystery. It is to be enjoyed and thought of as something of interest rather than a mystery. Armed with your favorite recipes, you can walk into a reputable wine store and turn a great meal into something wonderful.

One commonly used analogy to understand pairing is this; think about wine in relationship to a standard household item—milk. Wine can be classified by weight and most of us will understand this well, when comparing it to skim milk, 1%, 2%, whole milk, and cream. Think of your food and wine in terms of weight and you will be on the road to more interesting pairings. For example, a high-acid salad dressing, your homemade vinaigrette, needs a high-acid wine like Sauvignon Blanc. While vinaigrette can be light it is still high in acid. Chardonnay would be too "weighty" for vinaigrette and the acid in it would make the Chardonnay taste flat.

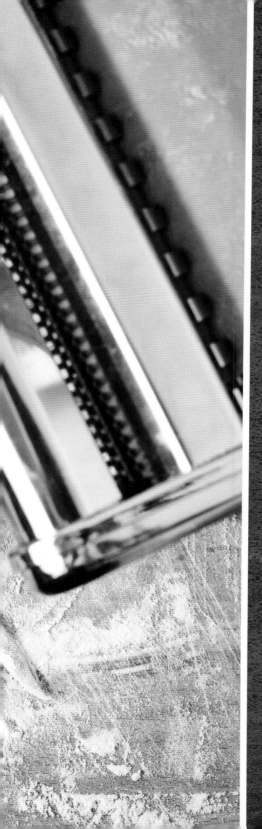

part 2
FOUNDATIONS

As a cookbook author and recipe developer, I believe that recipes should be versatile. If a recipe calls for cilantro and you or your family do not care for cilantro, you can substitute flat Italian parsley. Make notes in your cookbooks as to what you like or dislike and what you might change.

The recipes in this chapter are the "foundations" or basic recipes that can be tailored to your likes and dislikes. They can also be a starting place to customize your cooking. For example, simple pizza dough becomes any type of pizza that you like or it can also become focaccia or stromboli. A simply cooked spaghetti squash becomes different each time you change the sauce or topping.

So, go ahead, be creative and find your signature dish!

gnudi

The name gnudi or "naked pasta" is derived because this is similar to a ravioli filling and has no actual pasta around the filling. Thus the name "naked pasta." It is light and delicious and lower in carbs than most filled pastas.

---

1 (5-ounce) package baby spinach

2 cloves garlic

1 pound fat-free ricotta cheese

1/2 cup freshly grated Parmigiano-Reggiano cheese

1 egg white

1/2 cup white-wheat flour

1/2 teaspoon fine sea salt

1/4 teaspoon freshly cracked black pepper

1 | Place spinach and garlic cloves in food processor. Mince finely.

2 | Place ricotta in large bowl. Add spinach and garlic, Parmigiano, egg white, flour, salt, and pepper. Mix well by hand.

3 | Form 12 balls of ricotta mixture and place on a parchment-lined baking sheet. (Can be prepared ahead of time and refrigerated.)

4 | At cooking time, bring a large pot of water to a rolling boil. Drop Gnudi in the water. Once they float to the top, cook 2–3 minutes and serve with Fresh Tomato and Basil Sauce (page 44).

EXCHANGES/CHOICES
1/2 Carbohydrate
2 Protein, lean

CALORIES 125 | CALORIES FROM FAT 20
TOTAL FAT 2.0 g | SATURATED FAT 1.5 g | TRANS FAT 0.0 g
CHOLESTEROL 30 mg | SODIUM 310 mg | POTASSIUM 285 mg
TOTAL CARBOHYDRATE 11 g | DIETARY FIBER 2 g | SUGARS 3 g
PROTEIN 15 g | PHOSPHORUS 235 mg

GNUDI AND FRESH TOMATO AND BASIL SAUCE (page 44)

spaghetti squash

Spaghetti squash is a great way to cut down on complex carbs.

---

1 spaghetti squash (about 2 pounds)

1 | Wash spaghetti squash. Pierce with a fork in several places and place in microwave on high until skin is soft. This can take up to 30 minutes, but begin checking after 15 minutes. Let cool.

2 | Cut squash in half and remove seeds. To make "spaghetti." use a fork and pull out individual strands of "spaghetti."

3 | Top with Quick Fresh Herb Marinara Sauce (page 57) or toss with a sprinkling of garlic powder and Parmigiano-Reggiano cheese.

EXCHANGES/CHOICES
1 Vegetable

CALORIES 20 | CALORIES FROM FAT 0
TOTAL FAT 0.0 g | SATURATED FAT 0.0 g | TRANS FAT 0.0 g
CHOLESTEROL 0 mg | SODIUM 15 mg | POTASSIUM 90 mg
TOTAL CARBOHYDRATE 5 g | DIETARY FIBER 1 g | SUGARS 2 g
PROTEIN 1 g | PHOSPHORUS 10 mg

pizza dough

SERVES: 12 | SERVING SIZE: 1 SLICE

This recipe will yield 2–3 personal-size pizzas, one large pizza that will serve 12, 16 dinner rolls, or 12 sandwich rolls.

---

1 1/2 cups all-purpose flour

1 1/2 cups white-wheat flour

1 tablespoon active yeast

1 teaspoon fine sea salt

1–1 1/2 cups tepid water (water between 110–120°F)

1 teaspoon extra virgin olive oil

Chef's Secret

I use my food processor with steel blade to prepare the dough. The food processor does the kneading. Try to find the white whole-wheat flour, as it is lighter in color, texture, and taste than the traditional red whole-wheat flour.

Measure the temperature of the water with your meat thermometer. When working with yeast, water temperature is critical for proper rising. The correct temperature is 110–120 degrees.

1 | Place all dry ingredients in the bowl of your food processor. Pulse a few times to blend well.

2 | With the machine running, add 1 cup of water in a slow and steady stream. The dough should form a ball and the clean the sides of the food processor. If it seems too dry, add more water, 1 tablespoon at a time. The dough is perfect when it is no longer sticky and feels smooth. If it is too sticky or wet, you can add more flour 1 tablespoon at a time.

3 | Place dough in a large bowl with extra virgin olive oil. Turn dough to completely cover with oil and then cover tightly with plastic wrap and a cloth towel.

4 | Let dough rise in a warm place for at least one hour. A good place to rise is in the oven with the oven off and the oven light on.

5 | After the dough doubles in size, punch it down and let it rise again for as long as possible, at least one hour. I am a huge fan of the longer rise for lighter dough, especially when using whole-wheat flour.

EXCHANGES/CHOICES
1 1/2 Starch

CALORIES 115 | **CALORIES FROM FAT** 10
TOTAL FAT 1.0 g | **SATURATED FAT** 0.2 g | **TRANS FAT** 0.0 g
CHOLESTEROL 0 mg | **SODIUM** 185 mg | **POTASSIUM** 90 mg
TOTAL CARBOHYDRATE 21 g | **DIETARY FIBER** 2 g | **SUGARS** 0 g
PROTEIN 4 g | **PHOSPHORUS** 85 mg

how to
MAKE YOUR OWN PIZZA/CALZONE DOUGH

1   Mix yeast in tepid water. Let stand 5–10 minutes until foamy.

2   Set up food processor with steel blade (an electric mixer fitted with a dough hook also works well). Pour flour and salt into food processor. Pulse 2–3 times to mix salt and flour well.

3   Add yeast mixture and process until a ball forms inside the work bowl. Add 1 tablespoon extra virgin olive oil. Process 2 minutes. Dough should not be sticky. If it is, you can add more flour. Add the flour 1/4 cup at a time until dough is no longer sticky and does not stick to your hands.

4   Remove dough from work bowl and place on work surface that is lightly sprinkled with flour. Knead 3–5 minutes until dough is as soft as a baby's bottom. Place dough in a lightly oiled bowl and turn to coat all sides. Cover with plastic wrap and set in a warm place to rise. Dough should double in size within 1 or 2 hours.

5   Punch down and let rest for 10 minutes. Dough can also be given a second one hour rise for an even lighter pizza crust.

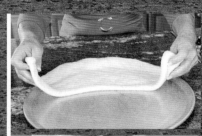

6   To avoid sticking, lightly sprinkle pan with cornmeal or line with parchment paper. If using a pizza peel to transfer pizza to stone, lightly sprinkle the peel with cornmeal. Stretch dough to desired size on pizza peel or prepared pan.

7   To cook pizza: Preheat oven and pizza stone to 500 degrees. Add toppings. Bake in preheated oven until outside edges of crust are golden and cheese is bubbly, approximately 15–20 minutes.

Variations

Grilled Pizza: *Preheat grill to high or 500°F. Flatten dough to desired size. Do not add toppings yet. Place flattened pizza dough directly onto grate and cook approximately 3–5 minutes with cover closed, or until grill marks appear and you are able to turn pizza dough with tongs. Turn dough and add toppings. Cook another 5 minutes or so with lid down.*

Toppings for grilled pizza should generally be light and can include fresh sliced tomatoes, fresh basil from your herb garden, and fresh mozzarella. You can also top your pizza with dollops of ricotta and homemade basil olive oil paste.

Chef's Secret

The moisture content in your flour and the atmosphere in your kitchen can vary greatly each time you make pizza. The best way to judge the dough is by the feel. It should feel smooth and not at all sticky.

Let pizza rest 5–10 minutes before cutting.

You can make pizza dough ahead and either let it rise all day in the refrigerator or freeze it.

A damp tea towel will also work in place of plastic wrap if you are placing your dough in a warm oven (less than 200°F) to rise. A hot, humid, summer day is great for rising. On top of a warm oven is also a good place to put dough to rise.

salad pizza

VINAIGRETTE

1/4 cup balsamic vinegar

Fine sea salt

Freshly ground pepper

1 clove garlic, zested

2 tablespoons extra virgin olive oil

1 recipe pizza dough (page 25)

3 cups baby greens

1/2 cup chopped plum tomatoes

2 scallions, sliced thinly on the diagonal

1/2 cup thinly sliced black olives

2 tablespoons finely chopped fresh mozzarella

1/4 cup freshly grated Parmigiano-Reggiano, Pecorino Romano, or Asiago

Red pepper flakes (optional)

1 | Whisk together vinegar, a pinch of sea salt, a grinding of pepper, and the garlic clove. Slowly whisk in olive oil to taste.

2 | Prepare individual pizza crusts (see page 25).

3 | Mix together greens, tomatoes, scallions, olives, and mozzarella. Toss with vinaigrette.

4 | Place salad ingredients on top of cooked pizza shell. Sprinkle with Parmigiano, Romano, or Asiago cheese. Sprinkle with optional red pepper flakes. Serve immediately.

Chef's Secret

To zest garlic, you can use your zester/grater.

EXCHANGES/CHOICES
1 1/2 Starch
1 1/2 Fat

CALORIES 180 | **CALORIES FROM FAT** 65
TOTAL FAT 7.0 g | **SATURATED FAT** 1.5 g | **TRANS FAT** 0.0 g
CHOLESTEROL 5 mg | **SODIUM** 260 mg | **POTASSIUM** 160 mg
TOTAL CARBOHYDRATE 23 g | **DIETARY FIBER** 3 g | **SUGARS** 1 g
PROTEIN 5 g | **PHOSPHORUS** 110 mg

how to
CHOP A TOMATO

1. Slice the tomato using a serrated knife. A serrated knife will not compress the flesh. Continue slicing tomato into wedges.

2. Depending on the size of the dice you need, you will continue slicing vertically.

3. To finish, cut horizontally.

stromboli with asiago and proscuitto

SERVES: 12 | SERVING SIZE: 1 SLICE

---

1 recipe pizza dough (page 25)

STROMBOLI FILLING

4 ounces proscuitto, thinly sliced

1 ounce Asiago D'Allevo DOP,
 coarsely grated

1 ounce Asiago Pressato DOP,
 coarsely grated

1 | Prepare pizza dough (page 25). Roll dough into rectangle. Layer prosciutto, Asiago D'Allevo DOP, and Asiago Pressato DOP. Roll jellyroll style. Pinch final seam. Brush with extra virgin olive oil for golden color. Can sprinkle additional cheese on top for taste and color.

2 | Bake at 375°F for 35–45 minutes or until golden. Cool at least 10 minutes before cutting.

EXCHANGES/CHOICES
2 Starch
1/2 Fat

CALORIES 185 | **CALORIES FROM FAT** 35
TOTAL FAT 4.0 g | **SATURATED FAT** 1.5 g | **TRANS FAT** 0.0 g
CHOLESTEROL 10 mg | **SODIUM** 245 mg | **POTASSIUM** 95 mg
TOTAL CARBOHYDRATE 28 g | **DIETARY FIBER** 1 g | **SUGARS** 0 g
PROTEIN 8 g | **PHOSPHORUS** 100 mg

STROMBOLI WITH ASIAGO AND PROSCUITTO

stromboli with gorgonzola and caramelized onions

SERVES: 12 | SERVING SIZE: 1 SLICE

1 recipe pizza dough (page 25)

STROMBOLI FILLING

1 recipe caramelized onions

3 ounces crumbled reduced-fat
Gorgonzola cheese

2 tablespoons fresh rosemary,
finely minced

1 | Prepare pizza dough (page 25). Roll dough into rectangle. Sprinkle with caramelized onions, Gorgonzola, and rosemary. Roll jellyroll style. Pinch final seam. Brush with extra virgin olive oil for golden color.

2 | Bake 375°F for 35–45 minutes or until golden. Cool at least 10 minutes before cutting.

EXCHANGES/CHOICES
2 Starch
1 Fat

CALORIES 195 | CALORIES FROM FAT 45
TOTAL FAT 5.0 g | SATURATED FAT 1.4 g | TRANS FAT 0.0 g
CHOLESTEROL 5 mg | SODIUM 125 mg | POTASSIUM 100 mg
TOTAL CARBOHYDRATE 30 g | DIETARY FIBER 2 g | SUGARS 1 g
PROTEIN 6 g | PHOSPHORUS 80 mg

fresh pasta

SERVES: 4 | SERVING SIZE: 1/2 CUP

Fresh pasta is worth the time. It is light and delicate and truly memorable. You can make fresh pasta from all-purpose flour or you can use a combination of white whole-wheat and all-purpose flour. I mix these together on the work surface before adding the eggs.

---

3 1/2 cups flour (all-purpose or a combination of white whole-wheat and all-purpose)

4 large eggs

Chef's Secret

To make a well in the flour, place the flour on your work surface and make a space for the eggs to be placed inside.

1 | Place the flour on a smooth work surface. If you have granite or marble countertops you can do it right on the countertop. Make a well in the mound of flour (See Chef's Secret, below). Add the eggs and break the yolks in the well. Begin moving flour to the well and incorporate it with the eggs. You will start with a sticky mess, but after kneading for 3–4 minutes it will become a smooth dough. It is also sometimes necessary to add a drop or two of water after the eggs have been incorporated to achieve a smooth consistency.

2 | Let the pasta dough rest for at least 20 minutes wrapped in plastic wrap at room temperature.

3 | The pasta dough can be passed though a pasta machine at this point. Fresh pasta takes very little time to cook. Add it to boiling water, wait for the water to come back to a boil, and the pasta floats to the top. It will take only 2–3 minutes to cook.

EXCHANGES/CHOICES
3 Starch

CALORIES 235 | CALORIES FROM FAT 25
TOTAL FAT 3.0 g | SATURATED FAT 0.9 g | TRANS FAT 0.0 g
CHOLESTEROL 95 mg | SODIUM 35 mg | POTASSIUM 95 mg
TOTAL CARBOHYDRATE 42 g | DIETARY FIBER 1 g | SUGARS 0 g
PROTEIN 9 g | PHOSPHORUS 110 mg

part 3
NO COOK

In this chapter, you will find very versatile recipes that do not require actual cooking. They are great recipes that range from salads, to salsas, to vinaigrettes, to sauces. Keep these in your repertoire to easily jazz up basic preparations like grilled chicken or fish. Vinaigrette can be used as a marinade or salad dressing. Pesto and salsas are handy to have on hand for unexpected company. Serve them with raw or roasted veggies, or low-fat cheeses. Save time by using these recipes to make leftovers special.

MAKE A VINAIGRETTE

1   Prepare *mise en place* (gather all ingredients).

4   Add seasonings.

2   Place vinegar in mixing bowl.

5   Blend well.

3   Slowly whisk in extra virgin olive oil.

Variations

Use different types and flavors of vinegar, lemon juice, or fruit juice for different dressings and marinades.

- Add 1–2 drops orange oil or orange extract
- Add chopped fresh herbs
- Add roasted garlic
- Fresh raspberries
- French vinaigrette: add 1 teaspoon Dijon mustard

basic vinaigrette

SERVES: 12 | SERVING SIZE: 1 TABLESPOON

This vinaigrette can be used as a salad dressing or as a marinade and tailored to your taste.

1/4 cup vinegar

Pinch fine sea salt

Freshly ground pepper, to taste

1/2 cup extra virgin olive oil

1 | Place vinegar, salt, and pepper in bowl. Start whisking and slowly stream in the olive oil.

EXCHANGES/CHOICES
2 Fat

CALORIES 80 | CALORIES FROM FAT 80
TOTAL FAT 9.0 g | SATURATED FAT 1.2 g | TRANS FAT 0.0 g
CHOLESTEROL 0 mg | SODIUM 15 mg | POTASSIUM 0 mg
TOTAL CARBOHYDRATE 0 g | DIETARY FIBER 0 g | SUGARS 0 g
PROTEIN 0 g | PHOSPHORUS 0 mg

raspberry vinaigrette

SERVES: 12 | SERVING SIZE: 1 TABLESPOON

1/4 cup champagne vinegar

Pinch fine sea salt

1/2 cup extra virgin olive oil

1/2 cup fresh raspberries

Freshly ground pepper, to taste

1 | Place vinegar and salt in bowl. Start whisking and slowly stream in the olive oil. Carefully fold in raspberries. Season with freshly ground pepper.

EXCHANGES/CHOICES
2 Fat

CALORIES 85 | CALORIES FROM FAT 80
TOTAL FAT 9.0 g | SATURATED FAT 1.2 g | TRANS FAT 0.0 g
CHOLESTEROL 0 mg | SODIUM 15 mg | POTASSIUM 10 mg
TOTAL CARBOHYDRATE 1 g | DIETARY FIBER 0 g | SUGARS 0 g
PROTEIN 0 g | PHOSPHORUS 0 mg

Chef's Secret

Slowly whisking in the oil allows for a better emulsion, meaning that the dressing will stay together longer. Best when prepared several hours ahead to allow the flavors to blend.

lemon vinaigrette

SERVES: 12 | SERVING SIZE: 1 TABLESPOON

This dressing will remind you of the higher-fat version known as Caesar dressing. Top with anchovies if desired.

1 lemon

1/4 cup freshly squeezed lemon juice

Pinch fine sea salt

1/2 cup extra virgin olive oil

Freshly ground pepper, to taste

2 tablespoons freshly grated
   Parmigiano-Reggiano cheese

1 small clove garlic, crushed, peeled,
   and minced (see How To Peel and
   Chop Garlic, page 46)

1 | Juice and zest the lemon.

2 | Place lemon juice, zest, and salt in bowl. Start whisking and slowly stream in the olive oil. Season with freshly ground pepper. Add Parmigiano and garlic.

Chef's Secret

Use a high-quality Parmigiano to add more flavor so that you can use less.

EXCHANGES/CHOICES
2 Fat

CALORIES 85 | CALORIES FROM FAT 80
TOTAL FAT 9.0 g | SATURATED FAT 1.4 g | TRANS FAT 0.0 g
CHOLESTEROL 0 mg | SODIUM 20 mg | POTASSIUM 10 mg
TOTAL CARBOHYDRATE 0 g | DIETARY FIBER 0 g | SUGARS 0 g
PROTEIN 0 g | PHOSPHORUS 5 mg

black bean and peach salsa

The dish is very colorful, which makes for a beautiful presentation. Use this as a dip or a side dish to any simply prepared protein. You can also toss with some greens for a great salad.

---

1 (15-ounce) can black beans, drained and rinsed

2 medium peaches, diced (about 2 cups)

1/2 teaspoon ground cumin

1 tablespoon extra virgin olive oil

1/2 cup chopped flat Italian parsley

2 fresh lemons, juiced

2 tablespoons minced red onion

1/8 teaspoon fine sea salt

Few grinds freshly ground pepper

1 | Mix all ingredients together. Prepare the salsa early in the day, if possible, to allow flavors to blend.

Chef's Secret

Mango can be substituted for the peach if you prefer.

EXCHANGES/CHOICES	
1/2 Carbohydrate	CALORIES 25	CALORIES FROM FAT 5

CALORIES 25 | CALORIES FROM FAT 5
TOTAL FAT 0.5 g | SATURATED FAT 0.1 g | TRANS FAT 0.0 g
CHOLESTEROL 0 mg | SODIUM 25 mg | POTASSIUM 70 mg
TOTAL CARBOHYDRATE 4 g | DIETARY FIBER 1 g | SUGARS 1 g
PROTEIN 1 g | PHOSPHORUS 20 mg

lemon garlic kale pesto

SERVES: 8 | SERVING SIZE: 2 TABLESPOONS

Baby kale is much more tender than the larger version and the taste is more delicate. Pesto simply means paste so you can make pesto out of anything. Use this as a dipping sauce, drizzle over a simply prepared protein, toss it with veggies, add it to a vinaigrette, or stir it into anything you like!

---

2 large cloves garlic, peeled

5 ounces baby kale (8 cups)

1/3 cup freshly squeezed lemon juice, about 2 lemons

1/2 teaspoon fine sea salt

1/2 teaspoon freshly milled black pepper

2 tablespoons extra virgin olive oil

1 | Place garlic in food processor fitted with steel blade. Pulse to chop.

2 | Add kale in several batches and process until fine after each addition. Stream in lemon juice, olive oil, salt, and pepper. Blend well.

3 | Store in airtight container several days or freeze.

EXCHANGES/CHOICES
1 Fat

CALORIES 45 | CALORIES FROM FAT 30
TOTAL FAT 3.5 g | SATURATED FAT 0.5 g | TRANS FAT 0.0 g
CHOLESTEROL 0 mg | SODIUM 145 mg | POTASSIUM 105 mg
TOTAL CARBOHYDRATE 3 g | DIETARY FIBER 1 g | SUGARS 2 g
PROTEIN 1 g | PHOSPHORUS 20 mg

garlic scape pesto

SERVES: 20 | SERVING SIZE: 1 TABLESPOON

Garlic scapes are the top part of the garlic that emerges early in the spring before the garlic is ready to be harvested. They are deliciously pungent and are a great addition to many dishes. Here I have created a pesto that you can keep in your fridge and use anytime you need to jazz up a quick dish.

---

8 ounces garlic scapes

2 tablespoons extra virgin olive oil

1/2 teaspoon fine sea salt

1/2 teaspoon freshly cracked black pepper

2 tablespoons water

1 | Cut scapes into 3–4-inch lengths and place in the bowl of your food processor fitted with a steel blade. Pulse a few times to chop.

2 | Add olive oil, salt, and pepper and process to a chunky paste. Add water and process to a finer paste. (More water can be added if a thinner consistency is desired.)

Chef's Secret

The texture of the garlic scape is such that the pesto will not be as fine as pesto made with basil.

EXCHANGES/CHOICES
Free food

CALORIES 15 | CALORIES FROM FAT 15
TOTAL FAT 1.5 g | SATURATED FAT 0.2 g | TRANS FAT 0.0 g
CHOLESTEROL 0 mg | SODIUM 55 mg | POTASSIUM 30 mg
TOTAL CARBOHYDRATE 1 g | DIETARY FIBER 0 g | SUGARS 0 g
PROTEIN 0 g | PHOSPHORUS 0 mg

guacamole

Guacamole is one of those things that is very, very easy to make. This is great when served with Sensational Chicken Burgers (page 129) or with baked chips.

2 avocados (purchase them soft), about 1 pound or 1 cup mashed

1 lime, juiced

2 tablespoons chopped tomato

2 tablespoons finely minced or grated onion

1 clove garlic, finely minced

1/4 cup chopped fresh cilantro or parsley

1/8 teaspoon fine sea salt

1 | Cut avocado in half and scoop flesh out with a spoon. Save pit. Place flesh in medium bowl and mash with fork.

2 | Add lime juice, tomato, onion, garlic, cilantro, and salt. Blend well. Place avocado pit back in the guacamole and cover it tightly to keep it from browning.

Chef's Secret

Use a box grater to grate a small onion for finely minced onion. Placing plastic wrap directly on the surface of the guacamole will also help to eliminate browning.

EXCHANGES/CHOICES
1 Fat

CALORIES 55 | CALORIES FROM FAT 45
TOTAL FAT 5.0 g | SATURATED FAT 0.7 g | TRANS FAT 0.0 g
CHOLESTEROL 0 mg | SODIUM 30 mg | POTASSIUM 175 mg
TOTAL CARBOHYDRATE 3 g | DIETARY FIBER 2 g | SUGARS 0 g
PROTEIN 1 g | PHOSPHORUS 20 mg

how to
CUT AN AVOCADO

1   Make a cut around the circumference of the avocado.

2   Twist the two halves so that they come apart.

3   One half will have the pit in the center.

4   Place your chef's knife in the pit and remove. It will come out easily.

5   Slide a spoon between the flesh and skin to remove flesh.

6   Slice or dice as necessary.

fresh tomato and basil sauce

SERVES: 16 | SERVING SIZE: 1/4 CUP

This sauce is great no matter what time of year you make it. If you want something cool in the summer, you don't even need to bother with cooking it. It will become more fragrant when tossed with hot, freshly cooked pasta.

---

12 plum tomatoes

1/2 teaspoon fine sea salt

2 cloves garlic

1 tablespoon extra virgin olive oil

1/4 teaspoon freshly ground pepper

1 cup fresh basil leaves

1 | Chop tomatoes into bite-sized pieces and place in medium bowl. Sprinkle with salt to bring out the flavor and juice. Let sit a few minutes. Meanwhile, finely mince the garlic. Add oil, garlic, and pepper to tomatoes.

2 | Tear basil leaves and add to tomato mixture.

3 | Serve fresh (uncooked) or sauté for 5–10 until tomatoes are softened.

EXCHANGES/CHOICES
Free food

CALORIES 15 | CALORIES FROM FAT 10
TOTAL FAT 1.0 g | SATURATED FAT 0.1 g | TRANS FAT 0.0 g
CHOLESTEROL 0 mg | SODIUM 70 mg | POTASSIUM 125 mg
TOTAL CARBOHYDRATE 2 g | DIETARY FIBER 1 g | SUGARS 1 g
PROTEIN 1 g | PHOSPHORUS 15 mg

spinach dip with basil and garlic

SERVES: 6 | SERVING SIZE: 2 TABLESPOONS

This recipe makes a very flavorful and really healthy low-fat dip or spread that your guests will not believe is so good for them!

---

1 cup fresh baby spinach

2 cloves garlic, minced

1 tablespoon minced shallot
(approximately 1 large)

1/4 cup grated Parmigiano-Reggiano
cheese

1/2 cup fresh basil

1 cup nonfat cottage cheese

2 teaspoons extra virgin olive oil

2 tablespoons skim milk (optional)

1 | Place spinach, garlic, shallot, Parmigiano-Reggiano, and basil in food processor. Process to a paste.

2 | With motor running, add cottage cheese and oil. Process until smooth. Add milk to achieve the desired consistency for your use.

Chef's Secret

Best when made a day ahead.

EXCHANGES/CHOICES
1 Protein, lean

CALORIES 60 | **CALORIES FROM FAT** 20
TOTAL FAT 2.5 g | **SATURATED FAT** 1.0 g | **TRANS FAT** 0.0 g
CHOLESTEROL 5 mg | **SODIUM** 150 mg | **POTASSIUM** 135 mg
TOTAL CARBOHYDRATE 4 g | **DIETARY FIBER** 0 g | **SUGARS** 1 g
PROTEIN 5 g | **PHOSPHORUS** 105 mg

how to
PEEL AND CHOP GARLIC

1   Place a head of garlic on work surface or cutting board.

3   Place a clove on cutting board and place chef's knife on top of clove. Firmly press on chef's knife and crush the clove of garlic.

5   Chop with chef's knife to desired size.

4   Remove papery skin.

2   Separate cloves.

white bean, herb, garlic, and lemon spread

SERVES: 10 | SERVING SIZE: 1/4 CUP

This dip is similar to hummus but I left out the tahini (sesame paste), which is almost all fat and can be costly and not readily available. It also has a brighter, fresher flavor since the garlic and lemon are more noticeable. Serve it as a dip for pita chips and raw vegetables or as a spread for bruschetta (page 63) or grilled vegetable sandwiches.

---

2 cups canned chickpeas or white beans, drained and rinsed well

2 cloves garlic, crushed and peeled

2 lemons, juiced

1 tablespoon extra virgin olive oil

1/2 teaspoon fine sea salt

1/4 teaspoon freshly ground pepper

1/4 cup chopped Italian parsley

1 tablespoon chopped fresh chives

1 | Mix all ingredients, except parsley and chives, in a food processor to make a smooth paste. Remove from food processor and stir in fresh herbs. (This recipe can be made up to two days ahead of time.)

Chef's Secret

To crush and peel garlic at the same time, you can place it on a cutting board and crush it with the side of a large chef's knife or a flat meat pounder.

EXCHANGES/CHOICES
1/2 Starch
1/2 Fat

CALORIES 65 | CALORIES FROM FAT 20
TOTAL FAT 2.0 g | SATURATED FAT 0.3 g | TRANS FAT 0.0 g
CHOLESTEROL 0 mg | SODIUM 165 mg | POTASSIUM 105 mg
TOTAL CARBOHYDRATE 9 g | DIETARY FIBER 2 g | SUGARS 2 g
PROTEIN 3 g | PHOSPHORUS 55 mg

baby kale salad with red onion, chickpeas, and black olives

SERVES: 4 | SERVING SIZE: 2 CUPS

I love making main dish salads. The chickpeas provide protein and the kale gives us all the benefits of our leafy greens. Add the red onion and olives for variety and you have a great salad. I also love using kale in salads because it is so substantial, it doesn't wilt like tender lettuces, and you can dress the salad ahead of time to let the flavors blend.

---

5 ounces baby kale (8 cups)

1 (15-ounce) can chickpeas (1 1/2 cups), drained

1/2 cup thinly sliced red onion

1 cup pitted black olives, rinsed and broken in half

1/4 teaspoon fine sea salt

1/2 teaspoon freshly milled black pepper

3 tablespoons red wine vinegar

1 1/2 tablespoons extra virgin olive oil

1/4 cup grated Parmigiano-Reggiano cheese

1 | Place kale in large salad bowl. Top with chickpeas, onion, and olives. Sprinkle with salt, pepper, vinegar, and olive oil. Toss well.

2 | Sprinkle with Parmigiano-Reggiano. Toss again and serve.

EXCHANGES/CHOICES
1 Starch
1 Vegetable
1 Protein, lean
2 Fat

CALORIES 230 | CALORIES FROM FAT 110
TOTAL FAT 12.0 g | SATURATED FAT 2.4 g | TRANS FAT 0.0 g
CHOLESTEROL 5 mg | SODIUM 545 mg | POTASSIUM 390 mg
TOTAL CARBOHYDRATE 24 g | DIETARY FIBER 7 g | SUGARS 7 g
PROTEIN 9 g | PHOSPHORUS 180 mg

how to
DICE AN ONION

3   Remove/peel outer layer of skin.

1   Place onion on work surface. Using a large chef's knife, cut onion in half from stem to root.

4   Place cut side down on work surface. Make horizontal cuts up to the root but not cutting through the root.

5   Make vertical cuts up to the root but not through the root.

2   Place cut side down on work surface. Remove (cut) stem end, leaving root end intact.

6   Slice across the top of onion.

fennel, red onion, and orange salad

SERVES: 4 | SERVING SIZE: 1 1/2 CUP

SALAD

1/2 cup thinly sliced fennel tops

1/2 medium red onion, thinly sliced

1 orange, peeled, cut in half, and
  thinly sliced

1/2 cup sliced cucumber

4 cups red leaf lettuce, washed,
  dried, and torn into bite-sized pieces
  (about 1 small head)

Orange slices for garnish

DRESSING

Juice of 1 orange

2 tablespoons extra virgin olive oil

1/4 teaspoon fine sea salt

1/4 teaspoon black pepper

1 tablespoon capers

1 | Whisk all dressing ingredients together.

2 | Place salad ingredients in large bowl. Toss with dressing.

EXCHANGES/CHOICES
1/2 Fruit
1 Vegetable
1 1/2 Fat

CALORIES 105 | CALORIES FROM FAT 65
TOTAL FAT 7.0 g | SATURATED FAT 1.0 g | TRANS FAT 0.0 g
CHOLESTEROL 0 mg | SODIUM 205 mg | POTASSIUM 240 mg
TOTAL CARBOHYDRATE 10 g | DIETARY FIBER 2 g | SUGARS 7 g
PROTEIN 1 g | PHOSPHORUS 30 mg

mexi-style salad

SERVES: 4 | SERVING SIZE: 1 CUP

Using a natural salsa as a salad dressing eliminates the need for oil-based dressing. This salad goes well with the Mexi-Style Meatballs (page 120).

---

4 cups baby salad greens

1/2 cup black bean and corn salsa

1/4 cup fat-free sharp cheddar cheese

1 | Place salad greens in large bowl. Top with salsa and cheese and toss well.

EXCHANGES/CHOICES
1/2 Carbohydrate

CALORIES 40 | CALORIES FROM FAT 0
TOTAL FAT 0.0 g | SATURATED FAT 0.0 g | TRANS FAT 0.0 g
CHOLESTEROL 0 mg | SODIUM 225 mg | POTASSIUM 255 mg
TOTAL CARBOHYDRATE 7 g | DIETARY FIBER 3 g | SUGARS 2 g
PROTEIN 4 g | PHOSPHORUS 60 mg

how to
CUT A MANGO

1   Place the mango on a cutting surface. You will notice that it is oval shaped. Make your first cut about 1/3 of the way toward center.

3   Begin scoring. The width of your cuts will determine the size of the dice.

5   Cut the pieces from the skin and use as needed.

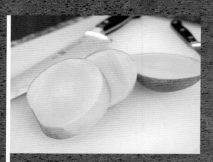

2   Repeat on the other side. You should now have 3 pieces (the center with pit and 2 sides).

4   Turn the mango inside out by pressing the skin up from the bottom.

mango chicken salad with jicama

SERVES: 4 | SERVING SIZE: 1 CUP

This refreshing salad has a surprise crunch from the diced jicama. The mango adds its own sweetness and lots of Vitamin C.

---

2 chicken breasts (16 ounces total), poached (page 73), cooled, and diced, or equivalent leftover roast or grilled chicken

1/4 cup finely minced red onion

1 large mango, diced into 1/4-inch pieces

1/2 cup jicama, diced into 1/4-inch pieces

1 cup roughly chopped cilantro

1 lime, juiced

6 ounces plain, low-fat Greek yogurt

Fine sea salt, to taste

Freshly ground pepper, to taste

4 cups mixed greens, washed and dried

1/2 cup toasted sunflower seeds, pumpkin seeds, or soy nuts for garnish

1 | Mix chicken, red onion, mango, jicama, cilantro, lime juice, and yogurt. Blend well. Add additional yogurt, as necessary, for desired consistency. Add salt and pepper to taste.

2 | Serve over mixed greens and garnish with additional mango, seeds, and cilantro.

Chef's Secret

This dish also makes a lovely hors d'oeuvre if placed in phyllo tart shells, which can be purchased at your supermarket.

EXCHANGES/CHOICES	
1 Fruit	CALORIES 320	CALORIES FROM FAT 110
1 Vegetable	TOTAL FAT 12.0 g	SATURATED FAT 2.1 g	TRANS FAT 0.0 g
4 Lean Meat	CHOLESTEROL 65 mg	SODIUM 85 mg	POTASSIUM 630 mg
1 Fat	TOTAL CARBOHYDRATE 22 g	DIETARY FIBER 5 g	SUGARS 14 g
	PROTEIN 33 g	PHOSPHORUS 410 mg

part 4
ON THE STOVETOP

Stovetop cooking can be fast and easy or long and slow. Either way, there are several methods you can use to cook "On the Stovetop."

SAUTÉ—the word sauté means to jump. To sauté, you need high heat and a good sauté or fry pan. You will place the item to be cooked, i.e. a thinly pounded chicken breast, in the pan and cook quickly over high heat for just a couple of minutes on each side until golden or crispy.

SEAR—Searing is quickly cooking a protein to seal in the juices. Once the protein has been "seared," it can be moved to the oven or liquid can be added to the pan to complete the cooking.

BOIL—In this book, boiling is the common method of cooking for pasta. To correctly cook pasta, place a large pot of water on the stove and bring the water to a "rolling" boil, which means large, rapid bubbles appear on the surface.

STEAM—Vegetables or seafood can be steamed either by using a steamer basket over a large pot with minimal water and a lid. I like to steam my vegetables to the crisp-tender stage so that I don't destroy all the vitamins and minerals.

POACH—Place the item to be poached in enough liquid so that it is completely submerged. The most common foods to be poached are eggs and chicken. To poach eggs: Crack the egg into a bowl and slowly and deliberately pour the egg into the simmering water for a few minutes. Chicken is placed in the liquid until cooked through, about 9–10 minutes for a boneless, skinless breast. (See Poached Chicken, page 73. There is also a recipe for Poached Arctic Char, page 76.)

STIR FRY—Most commonly thought of with regard to Asian cooking, stir frying is another method of quick cooking over high heat with a small amount of oil or liquid. (See How to Stir-Fry, page 89.)

balsamic glaze for drizzling

SERVES: 8 | SERVING SIZE: 1 TABLESPOON

The balsamic drizzle is a finishing touch that comes in handy for finishing many of the dishes in this book, such as the Grilled Vegetables (page 126) or any grilled protein. Be sure to select balsamic vinegar that is imported from Modena, Italy, and has no additives such as caramel color or flavor.

---

1 cup balsamic vinegar

1 | Place vinegar in small saucepan and simmer for 15–20 minutes until reduced to 1/2 cup.

EXCHANGES/CHOICES
1/2 Carbohydrate

CALORIES 25 | CALORIES FROM FAT 0
TOTAL FAT 0.0 g | SATURATED FAT 0.0 g | TRANS FAT 0.0 g
CHOLESTEROL 0 mg | SODIUM 5 mg | POTASSIUM 35 mg
TOTAL CARBOHYDRATE 5 g | DIETARY FIBER 0 g | SUGARS 4 g
PROTEIN 0 g | PHOSPHORUS 5 mg

warm shallot vinaigrette

SERVES: 6 | SERVING SIZE: 1 TABLESPOON

A warm vinaigrette is a wonderful change of pace. It will also slightly wilt tender greens for a contrast in texture.

---

3 tablespoons olive oil

2 tablespoons white wine vinegar

2 teaspoons honey

1 chopped shallot

1 | Heat olive oil in a small saucepan. Add white wine vinegar, honey, and shallot. Mix well and keep warm until serving time.

EXCHANGES/CHOICES
1 1/2 Fat

CALORIES 70 | CALORIES FROM FAT 65
TOTAL FAT 7.0 g | SATURATED FAT 0.9 g | TRANS FAT 0.0 g
CHOLESTEROL 0 mg | SODIUM 0 mg | POTASSIUM 15 mg
TOTAL CARBOHYDRATE 3 g | DIETARY FIBER 0 g | SUGARS 2 g
PROTEIN 0 g | PHOSPHORUS 0 mg

quick fresh herb marinara sauce

SERVES: 4 | SERVING SIZE: 1/2 CUP

This quick sauce is so handy you will want to have the ingredients on hand at all times. Marjoram is a more delicate than oregano and I prefer it whenever I can get it.

---

1 tablespoon extra virgin olive oil

4 cloves garlic, minced

1/2 cup chopped fresh basil

1/2 cup chopped marjoram or oregano

28 ounces diced canned tomatoes or
  12 fresh plum tomatoes, chopped

1/4 teaspoon fine sea salt

Freshly ground pepper

Additional basil, as desired

1 | Lightly film a 10–12-inch sauté pan with olive oil and heat over medium heat.

2 | Add garlic and cook until fragrant. When garlic is golden brown, add basil, oregano, and tomatoes. Simmer 20 minutes. If meatballs are to be added, you can add them at this point.

3 | Add sea salt and pepper. Add more basil if desired. Simmer 10 minutes more or longer.

Chef's Secret

This is suitable for pizza sauce, pasta sauce, and to simmer any meatballs.

EXCHANGES/CHOICES	
2 Vegetable	
1/2 Fat	

CALORIES 75 | CALORIES FROM FAT 35
TOTAL FAT 4.0 g | SATURATED FAT 0.5 g | TRANS FAT 0.0 g
CHOLESTEROL 0 mg | SODIUM 425 mg | POTASSIUM 450 mg
TOTAL CARBOHYDRATE 10 g | DIETARY FIBER 3 g | SUGARS 5 g
PROTEIN 2 g | PHOSPHORUS 50 mg

mushroom sherry sauce

SERVES: 6 | SERVING SIZE: 1/4 CUP

This wonderful sauce is very versatile and can be used on anything! The type of stock and wine can also be varied according to what you are serving this with.

2 tablespoons extra virgin olive oil

1 shallot, minced, or 2 cloves garlic, minced

10 ounces mushrooms, sliced

2 tablespoons flour

1/2 –1 cup vegetable stock

1/2 cup dry sherry or wine

1/2 cup Italian parsley, minced

1 | Place olive oil in sauté pan. Add shallot and mushrooms and cook until wilted.

2 | Add flour and cook 3 minutes.

3 | Add stock and sherry or wine and reduce sauce to desired consistency, about 10–15 minutes. Add fresh parsley.

EXCHANGES/CHOICES
1/2 Carbohydrate
1 Fat

CALORIES 75 | CALORIES FROM FAT 40
TOTAL FAT 4.5 g | SATURATED FAT 0.6 g | TRANS FAT 0.0 g
CHOLESTEROL 0 mg | SODIUM 85 mg | POTASSIUM 230 mg
TOTAL CARBOHYDRATE 5 g | DIETARY FIBER 1 g | SUGARS 1 g
PROTEIN 2 g | PHOSPHORUS 55 mg

how to
COOK WITH WINE

One of the ways to add great flavor to dishes and cut down on fat is to cook with wine. When wine is reduced in your dish, it concentrates flavor. When cutting down on the fats used in your cooking, wine is another vehicle for delivering flavor.

Cook with wine that is also drinkable. This way, when you decide on a recipe that requires wine, you should select a wine that is good enough to enjoy drinking. A common mistake that people make is to go to the wine shop and purchase the least expensive red or white they can find. The wine that you will be serving for dinner should complement the food that you are serving so you should cook with the same type of wine you would be serving with the meal. If you are cooking with a dry Italian red, you want to serve a similar wine with the meal.

For those who don't generally keep wine in the house, white vermouth is a good choice for cooking because it is made with a blend of savory herbs. Wine can be used in place of fats, but it can also be added to deglaze a pan that has been used to brown, sear, or caramelize foods prior to creating a sauce. The little bits of food that are stuck to the pan are called fond; these bits are quickly and easily lifted when you add a splash of wine (or any liquid) to the hot pan. This creates the basis for your sauce and adds a great deal of flavor to the dish. It is also a good idea to remove the pan from the heat while doing this. Research has indicated that 98–99% of the alcohol cooks out of the dish.

WARM KALE CAESAR STYLE SALAD WITH CRAB

how to

TOAST PIGNOLI NUTS

| 1 | Place pignoli nuts in dry skillet over medium heat. |

| 2 | Watch carefully and stir until golden. |

| 3 | Nuts have volatile oils so once golden, they are done. Remove from pan to prevent overcooking or burning. |

warm kale caesar style salad with crab

SERVES: 2 | SERVING SIZE: 2 CUPS KALE AND 2 OUNCES CRAB

Warm salad dressing will slightly wilt the greens and completely change a humdrum salad into something special.

1 tablespoon plus 1 teaspoon extra virgin olive oil

2 cloves garlic, thinly sliced

1 lemon, juiced

1/2 cup chopped fresh basil

1/4 teaspoon fine sea salt

1/2 teaspoon freshly ground black pepper

1 (5-ounce) bag baby kale (8 cups)

2 Cerignola olives, pitted and sliced

2 tablespoons toasted pignoli (pine) nuts

2 tablespoons pomegranate arils (seeds)

2–3 radishes, sliced

4 ounces lump crabmeat

1 | Place olive oil in a small saucepan. Add garlic and cook until it begins to brown around the edges. Add the lemon juice, basil, salt, and pepper. Keep warm while assembling salad.

2 | Place kale in large salad bowl. Top with olives, pignoli nuts, pomegranate, and radishes. Add dressing and toss well. Divide between two dinner plates and top with crabmeat.

Chef's Secret

The seeds of the pomegranate are actually called arils. Some markets sell packages of arils to save you the time and trouble of removing them from the pomegranate.

EXCHANGES/CHOICES
2 Vegetable
2 Protein, lean
3 Fat

CALORIES 275 | CALORIES FROM FAT 180
TOTAL FAT 20.0 g | SATURATED FAT 2.3 g | TRANS FAT 0.0 g
CHOLESTEROL 75 mg | SODIUM 575 mg | POTASSIUM 720 mg
TOTAL CARBOHYDRATE 13 g | DIETARY FIBER 3 g | SUGARS 8 g
PROTEIN 15 g | PHOSPHORUS 265 mg

zucchini and tomato mix

SERVES: 8 | SERVING SIZE: 1/3 CUP

This mixture makes a great sauce for pasta, grilled proteins, or a bruschetta topping.

---

1 tablespoon extra virgin olive oil

2 cloves garlic, finely minced

1 medium zucchini, sliced
  (about 2 cups)

4 plum tomatoes

1/2 teaspoon fine sea salt

1/4 teaspoon freshly ground pepper

1 cup fresh basil leaves

1 | Place olive oil in large sauté pan. Add garlic and zucchini and cook until zucchini begin to wilt. Add tomatoes. Remove pan from heat. Stir in salt, pepper, and fresh basil.

EXCHANGES/CHOICES
1 Vegetable

CALORIES 25 | **CALORIES FROM FAT** 20
TOTAL FAT 2.0 g | **SATURATED FAT** 0.3 g | **TRANS FAT** 0.0 g
CHOLESTEROL 0 mg | **SODIUM** 140 mg | **POTASSIUM** 165 mg
TOTAL CARBOHYDRATE 3 g | **DIETARY FIBER** 1 g | **SUGARS** 1 g
PROTEIN 1 g | **PHOSPHORUS** 20 mg

how to
TOAST BRUSCHETTA

There are several recipes in this book that refer to bruschetta. Bruschetta comes from the Italian word "bruscare", which means "to char." The grilled bread is the bruschetta, not the toppings, which is a common misunderstanding. There are a variety of toppings you can use on bruschetta; however the most common is a simple mix of tomatoes and basil.

1   Slice a loaf of whole-grain Italian bread.

3   Place bread slices on a grill top or grill pan and grill on medium heat until grill marks appear.

2   Brush it lightly with extra virgin olive oil.

4   Place grilled slices on a platter and top with your favorite topping. Tomato and basil are the classic toppings for bruschetta but there is an endless variety of possibilities.

portobello mushrooms and onions with balsamic glaze

SERVES: 15 | SERVING SIZE: 1 OUNCE

This sautéed mushroom mixture is great as a bruschetta topping, a side dish for a grilled protein, or a pasta topping.

2 teaspoons olive oil

2 cups onion, thinly sliced

2 garlic cloves, minced

6 portobello mushrooms,
 sliced 1/4-inch thick

Fine sea salt, to taste

Freshly ground pepper, to taste

Crushed red pepper, to taste (optional)

3/4 cup balsamic vinegar

1 | Heat a sauté pan and thinly film with olive oil. Add onion, garlic, and mushrooms. Cook until soft and onions are translucent. Add salt and pepper to taste and red pepper, if desired. Can also be done a day ahead and reheated or brought to room temperature before serving.

2 | Heat balsamic vinegar in a small saucepan, bring to a boil, and then reduce to low. Cook until syrupy or the vinegar lightly coats the back of a spoon. This will take approximately 20 minutes. Set aside.

3 | Spread mushroom mixture on grilled bread. Drizzle with reduced balsamic vinegar. Can be served as an appetizer or hors d'oeuvre.

Chef's Secret

You can substitute garlic paste in this recipe if you are cooking for someone who doesn't like actual bits of garlic in their food. (See How To Make Garlic Paste, page 65).

EXCHANGES/CHOICES
1/2 Carbohydrate

CALORIES 30 | **CALORIES FROM FAT** 5
TOTAL FAT 0.5 g | **SATURATED FAT** 0.1 g | **TRANS FAT** 0.0 g
CHOLESTEROL 0 mg | **SODIUM** 5 mg | **POTASSIUM** 170 mg
TOTAL CARBOHYDRATE 5 g | **DIETARY FIBER** 0 g | **SUGARS** 3 g
PROTEIN 1 g | **PHOSPHORUS** 40 mg

how to
MAKE GARLIC PASTE

If you don't like actual bits of garlic in your food, try this tip for making garlic into a paste. This technique gives you the wonderful flavor of garlic, without the chopped up bits.

1   Chop garlic and add a pinch of salt. Using your chef's knife, continue to crush the garlic and salt together.

2   Continue until you have the desired consistency. (The more you use your knife, the finer the paste.)

fava with lemon and garlic

SERVES: 32 | SERVING SIZE: 2 TABLESPOONS

Fava beans are a wonderful spring vegetable, but this recipe calls for dried fava so you can enjoy it anytime. I've turned this into a very healthy dip for your next party, but it can be served as a bruschetta topping or as a side dish with many of the recipes in this book.

1 small onion, finely diced
(about 1/2 cup)

2 cloves garlic, minced

3/4 pound dried, skinless fava beans

1 teaspoon fine sea salt

1/2 teaspoon freshly ground
black pepper

Juice of 2 lemons (about 1/3 cup)

Chef's Secret

To serve, place in low bowl and garnish with chopped tomato and basil. You could also divide this into two dips by putting the lemon in one half and some crushed red pepper in the other half.

1 | Place diced onion and garlic on bottom of medium saucepan. Pour fava on top.

2 | Cover fava with water just to the surface of the fava. (Additional water may be needed during the cooking process. You want the fava to be covered with water until they begin to break up.) It will take about 20–30 minutes to cook thoroughly.

3 | Bring pan to a boil. Reduce heat, cover, and simmer until fava are tender and they begin to break up. (Add additional water if needed.) Once tender, you can cook until the water has been absorbed. Allow a few minutes to cool.

4 | Purée contents in your food processor or with a hand blender to consistency of mashed potatoes or hummus. Add salt, pepper, and lemon.

EXCHANGES/CHOICES
1/2 Starch

CALORIES 35 | CALORIES FROM FAT 0
TOTAL FAT 0.0 g | SATURATED FAT 0.0 g | TRANS FAT 0.0 g
CHOLESTEROL 0 mg | SODIUM 70 mg | POTASSIUM 90 mg
TOTAL CARBOHYDRATE 6 g | DIETARY FIBER 2 g | SUGARS 1 g
PROTEIN 2 g | PHOSPHORUS 40 mg

mashed potatoes with no cream or butter

SERVES: 12 | SERVING SIZE: 1/2 CUP

This low-fat version of mashed potatoes can be made into garlic mashed potatoes by adding 3–4 cloves of garlic to the potatoes while cooking, or can be made vegetarian by using vegetable stock.

---

3 pounds Yukon gold potatoes, peeled and cut into 1-inch cubes

1 teaspoon fine sea salt

Freshly ground pepper, to taste

4 cups chicken, vegetable, or beef stock

1 | Place potatoes, salt, and pepper in heavy saucepan. Add stock and enough water to completely cover potatoes. Boil until potatoes are fork tender, at least 15 minutes.

2 | Drain liquid from potatoes into a bowl, reserving liquid to add back to potatoes later.

3 | Place potatoes in mixer bowl. Mix until smooth and add the hot cooking liquid until potatoes are desired consistency.

Chef's Secret

Leftover cooking liquid can be used in sauces or soups. These potatoes can be frozen in an ovenproof casserole dish, defrosted, and reheated in a 350°F oven until piping hot, approximately 45 minutes.

EXCHANGES/CHOICES
1 Starch

CALORIES 75 | CALORIES FROM FAT 0
TOTAL FAT 0.0 g | SATURATED FAT 0.0 g | TRANS FAT 0.0 g
CHOLESTEROL 0 mg | SODIUM 130 mg | POTASSIUM 295 mg
TOTAL CARBOHYDRATE 18 g | DIETARY FIBER 2 g | SUGARS 1 g
PROTEIN 2 g | PHOSPHORUS 35 mg

CAULIFLOWER SOUP WITH PROSCIUTTO CRISPS AND BLUE CHEESE SPRINKLE

cauliflower soup with prosciutto crisps and blue cheese sprinkle

SERVES: 12 | SERVING SIZE: 1/2 CUP

Cauliflower works well with bold flavors because it is like a fresh, blank canvas. You can also prepare the basic soup and garnish it with your favorite ingredients. Parmigiano-Reggiano would be a nice complement if you are not a fan of blue cheese.

---

2 tablespoons extra virgin olive oil

1 cup chopped onion (about 1 medium)

1 clove garlic, chopped

1 cup chopped celery, about 2 stalks

1 head cauliflower (about 36 ounces when purchased, 24 ounces after trimming, 7 cups chopped)

4 ounces prosciutto

1/2 teaspoon fine sea salt

2 cups low-sodium vegetable broth

2 cups water

1 cup evaporated skim milk

8 teaspoons blue cheese powder

1 | Place olive oil in 6- or 8-quart soup pot. Add onions, garlic, celery, and cauliflower and sauté approximately 5 minutes. Cover and cook until tender, about 10 minutes.

2 | Place prosciutto slices on parchment-lined baking sheet and bake in 400°F oven until crisp, about 10 minutes. Set aside for garnish.

3 | Add salt, stock, and water to the cauliflower mixture and cook 10 minutes. Add evaporated skim milk and heat thoroughly. Purée with stick blender, food processor, or blender. If using a food processor or blender, make sure that you leave some room for steam to escape by removing the small cap. Cover with a dishtowel. Process until smooth.

4 | Return to pan and heat thoroughly. Place 1 cup soup in bowl and top with a prosciutto crisp and a teaspoon of blue cheese powder and serve immediately.

EXCHANGES/CHOICES
2 Vegetable
1 Protein, lean
1 Fat

CALORIES 130 | CALORIES FROM FAT 55
TOTAL FAT 6.0 g | SATURATED FAT 1.7 g | TRANS FAT 0.0 g
CHOLESTEROL 10 mg | SODIUM 535 mg | POTASSIUM 520 mg
TOTAL CARBOHYDRATE 12 g | DIETARY FIBER 2 g | SUGARS 7 g
PROTEIN 9 g | PHOSPHORUS 175 mg

farro soup with mushrooms and kale

SERVES: 10 | SERVING SIZE: 1 CUP

Often mistaken for wheat, farro is actually a descendent of emmer. It is an ancient grain now grown in Italy, with a high fiber content and it is low in gluten. It has a lot of crunch and performs a lot like arborio rice in risotto but retains its distinct crunch. It is rich in fiber, magnesium, and Vitamins A, B, C, and E.

2 tablespoons extra virgin olive oil

1 cup diced onion (5-ounce onion or 1/2 of a large onion)

1 cup sliced carrots

1 cup sliced celery

2 cups sliced mushroom (8-ounce package)

2 cups uncooked farro (about 12 ounces)

1 teaspoon Stress Free Cooking Italian Blend (page 9)

1/2 teaspoon Stress Free Cooking Seasoning Blend (page 9)

32 ounces low-sodium vegetable stock

6 cups water

8 cups chopped kale, about 1/2 pound

Crushed red pepper (optional)

Cheese rinds (optional)

1 | Place olive oil in large soup pot. Add onion and cook until edges begin to brown. Add carrots, celery, and mushrooms and sauté vegetables 3–4 minutes for added flavor and color.

2 | Add farro and mix well with vegetables. Add Stress Free Cooking Italian Seasoning Blend and Stress Free Cooking Seasoning Blend. Mix well.

3 | Add stock, water, and rind. Bring to boil and then reduce to simmer. Cook 20 minutes. Add kale and cook an additional 5–10 minutes to tenderize kale. Serve.

Chef's Secret

The leftover rind of a piece of a Parmigiano-Reggiano or Grana Padano cheese will add a lot of flavor without a lot of calories. The crushed red pepper will provide a little kick to the savory grains and kale.

EXCHANGES/CHOICES
1 1/2 Starch
1 Vegetable
1/2 Fat

CALORIES 155 | CALORIES FROM FAT 35
TOTAL FAT 4.0 g | SATURATED FAT 0.6 g | TRANS FAT 0.0 g
CHOLESTEROL 0 mg | SODIUM 175 mg | POTASSIUM 445 mg
TOTAL CARBOHYDRATE 27 g | DIETARY FIBER 8 g | SUGARS 5 g
PROTEIN 7 g | PHOSPHORUS 180 mg

minestrone soup

SERVES: 20 | SERVING SIZE: 1 CUP

Minestrone means "big soup" in Italian. This soup is also a great comfort food to bring to friends and neighbors. Adding a piece of rind of good quality Parmigiano-Reggiano or Grana Padano cheese will add flavor without a lot of calories. Keep them in your freezer to add to soups and sauces.

2 tablespoons extra virgin olive oil

2 cups chopped onion (about 1 large)

4 large cloves garlic, minced

2 cups sliced celery

2 cups sliced carrots

4 cups quartered and thinly sliced zucchini or yellow squash or a combination of both

56 ounces canned diced tomatoes

4 cups low-sodium chicken or vegetable stock

4 cups water

2 cups of canned small white beans or chickpeas, drained and rinsed well

Rind from Parmigiano-Reggiano or Grana Padano (optional)

3 cups uncooked small pasta (such as ditalini or acini di pepe)

1 cup fresh basil, roughly chopped

1/2 cup fresh oregano, finely chopped

4 bay leaves

1 teaspoon fine sea salt

Freshly ground pepper, to taste

1 (5-ounce) bag baby arugula

1 | Place olive oil in large soup pot. Add onion and cook until it begins to brown. Add garlic, celery, and carrots. Sauté 3–5 minutes but do not let garlic get dark brown or black.

2 | Add zucchini, tomatoes, stock, water, beans, and cheese rind. Cook until vegetables are tender, 10–15 minutes.

3 | Add pasta, herbs, salt, and a few grindings of pepper. Cook until pasta is al dente, approximately 15–20 minutes. Add arugula during the last 2–3 minutes of cooking time. Stir well. Remove bay leaves before serving.

4 | Serve with a sprinkle of freshly grated Parmigiano-Reggiano, a mixed green salad, and crusty bread for a satisfying meal.

Chef's Secrets

When you buy a piece of Parmigiano-Reggiano or Grana Padano, save the rind and use it in soups or sauces for a low-calorie way to add the flavor of cheese to the dish.

Remove the bay leaves before serving. They are sharp and can cause injury if swallowed.

Since this is such a "big" soup, you might find that you want to add more water to achieve desired consistency.

Rinsing the beans also eliminates any gas from the beans.

EXCHANGES/CHOICES	
1 1/2 Starch	
2 Vegetable	

CALORIES 170 | CALORIES FROM FAT 20
TOTAL FAT 2.0 g | SATURATED FAT 0.3 g | TRANS FAT 0.0 g
CHOLESTEROL 0 mg | SODIUM 390 mg | POTASSIUM 510 mg
TOTAL CARBOHYDRATE 32 g | DIETARY FIBER 5 g | SUGARS 5 g
PROTEIN 7 g | PHOSPHORUS 125 mg

mushroom wild rice soup

SERVES: 10 | SERVING SIZE: 1 CUP

Mushrooms are low in calories so they are a given for healthy cooking. I like to add the wild rice to this soup to round it out.

4 ounces diced pancetta

1 teaspoon extra virgin olive oil

1 cup diced onion (about 1 medium)

3 cloves garlic, minced

2 carrots, sliced (about 1 cup)

2 stalks celery, sliced (about 1 cup)

24 ounces mushrooms, sliced

1 cup uncooked wild rice

1 envelope chicken broth concentrate

2 quarts water

1 cup fresh parsley, chopped

1/2 cup fresh basil, chopped

1 teaspoon Worcestershire sauce

1 | Place pancetta and olive oil in 6- or 8-quart soup pot. Brown the pancetta. Add onion and garlic and cook until onion is translucent.

2 | Add carrots, celery, and mushrooms and cook until mushrooms begin to brown.

3 | Add rice, broth concentrate, water, parsley, basil, and Worcestershire. Bring to a boil. Reduce heat to low and cook until rice is tender, about 45 minutes.

EXCHANGES/CHOICES
1 Starch
1 Vegetable
1 Fat

CALORIES 135 | CALORIES FROM FAT 45
TOTAL FAT 5.0 g | SATURATED FAT 1.4 g | TRANS FAT 0.0 g
CHOLESTEROL 10 mg | SODIUM 330 mg | POTASSIUM 480 mg
TOTAL CARBOHYDRATE 18 g | DIETARY FIBER 3 g | SUGARS 3 g
PROTEIN 7 g | PHOSPHORUS 200 mg

poached chicken

SERVES: 4 | SERVING SIZE: 4 OUNCES

Knowing how to poach chicken is very handy for healthy cooking. If you have some poached chicken in your fridge, you can use it so many ways. In this book, you will find poached chicken used in several recipes.

4 boneless, skinless chicken breasts
  (4 ounces each)

1 carrot

1 stalk celery

1 bay leaf

2 quarts water or chicken stock

1 | Place chicken, carrot, celery, and bay leaf in sauté pan and add enough stock or water to completely cover chicken and bring to low boil.

2 | Reduce heat to low and cook 8–10 minutes.

3 | Cool chicken in water or stock and prepare as necessary for the desired recipe. (Make sure to remove bay leaf before serving.)

EXCHANGES/CHOICES
3 Protein, lean

CALORIES 125 | CALORIES FROM FAT 20
TOTAL FAT 2.5 g | SATURATED FAT 0.7 g | TRANS FAT 0.0 g
CHOLESTEROL 65 mg | SODIUM 55 mg | POTASSIUM 160 mg
TOTAL CARBOHYDRATE 0 g | DIETARY FIBER 0 g | SUGARS 0 g
PROTEIN 24 g | PHOSPHORUS 140 mg

how to
FLATTEN CHICKEN BREASTS

Pounding the chicken breast allows it to cook more evenly.

1   Place chicken breast in plastic bag or folded parchment paper.

3   Continue pounding until you have desired thickness.

2   Using a flat meat pounder, begin in the center and pound toward the outer edges.

lemon chicken with capers

SERVES: 4 | SERVING SIZE: 4 OUNCES

A classic restaurant dish that is easy to make at home.

---

1 pound boneless, skinless
chicken breasts

1/4 cup Wondra flour

1/2 teaspoon fine sea salt

1/4 teaspoon ground pepper

1 tablespoon extra virgin olive oil

3 cloves garlic, minced

1 cup dry white vermouth or
dry white wine

Juice of 1 lemon

1/4 cup capers

1/4 cup chopped fresh basil

1 lemon, sliced thinly into rounds

1 | Pound chicken to 1/4-inch thickness (see How To Flatten Chicken Breasts page 74). Set aside.

2 | Place flour in large bowl and season with salt and pepper. Coat chicken with flour mixture.

3 | Place olive oil in large sauté pan and heat. Add chicken and brown first side. Turn chicken and brown other side. Add garlic in between chicken pieces.

4 | When chicken is golden on both sides, add vermouth and lemon juice. Turn heat to low and add capers and basil. Add lemon slices and simmer 10 minutes. Serve over 8 ounces spinach linguine.

Chef's Secret

Wondra, commonly known as instant flour, is very fine granular flour that is also used to make smooth sauces. All-purpose flour can be substituted.

EXCHANGES/CHOICES
1 Carbohydrate
3 Protein, lean

CALORIES 220 | **CALORIES FROM FAT** 55
TOTAL FAT 6.0 g | **SATURATED FAT** 1.3 g | **TRANS FAT** 0.0 g
CHOLESTEROL 65 mg | **SODIUM** 570 mg | **POTASSIUM** 315 mg
TOTAL CARBOHYDRATE 12 g | **DIETARY FIBER** 2 g | **SUGARS** 1 g
PROTEIN 26 g | **PHOSPHORUS** 200 mg

arctic char poached with white wine, lemon, and rosemary

SERVES: 4 | SERVING SIZE: 4 OUNCES

Arctic char is a wonderfully sweet, pink-fleshed fish that is a cousin to salmon and trout. It is slightly larger than a trout and sweeter than salmon. This fish is exceptionally pleasing to those who find salmon a bit strong.

---

2 cups dry white wine, such as Sauvignon Blanc or Pinot Grigio (or fish stock)

4 sprigs fresh rosemary

1/4 teaspoon fine sea salt

Freshly ground pepper to taste

2 fresh lemons

1 pound arctic char fillet, skin removed

Additional rosemary for garnish

1 | Place wine or stock, rosemary, salt, a few grinds of black pepper, and slices of one lemon in a sauté pan.

2 | Add fish to pan. Bring to low boil, cover, and simmer until fish is done, approximately 10 minutes.

3 | Serve with additional lemon slices and sprigs of rosemary.

Chef's Secret

You can ask your seafood manager to skin the fish for you. This cooking method will work for any fish. The rule of thumb is to cook fish for 10 minutes per inch of thickness.

EXCHANGES/CHOICES
4 Protein, lean

CALORIES 170 | CALORIES FROM FAT 65
TOTAL FAT 7.0 g | SATURATED FAT 1.4 g | TRANS FAT 0.0 g
CHOLESTEROL 50 mg | SODIUM 80 mg | POTASSIUM 415 mg
TOTAL CARBOHYDRATE 0 g | DIETARY FIBER 0 g | SUGARS 0 g
PROTEIN 24 g | PHOSPHORUS 265 mg

halibut with white beans in tomato basil broth

SERVES: 4 | SERVING SIZE: 4 OUNCES FISH AND 1 1/2 CUPS BEANS AND BROTH

Not only are the beans a healthy addition to this dish, but they also will help absorb some of the delicious broth so you won't miss a drop.

2 teaspoons extra virgin olive oil

1 pound halibut fillet

1/4 teaspoon fine sea salt

1/4 teaspoon freshly ground black pepper

2 cloves garlic, crushed and chopped

2 (15-ounce) cans small white beans, drained and rinsed

2 cups chopped fresh plum tomatoes (about 6)

1/2 cup fresh basil leaves, torn

1 cup white wine or low-sodium, low-fat chicken stock

1 cup low-sodium, low-fat chicken stock

1 | Place olive oil in large skillet. Heat skillet to medium-high heat and add fish. Sprinkle fish with salt and pepper and sprinkle garlic directly onto pan surface. Cook 3 minutes, then turn fish with large turner.

2 | Add beans, tomatoes, basil, wine, and stock. Cover and cook until fish is tender and begins to flake, approximately 5 minutes.

3 | Place fish in large bowl with plenty of tomato basil broth.

Chef's Secret

If fresh tomatoes are out of season or you don't have any in the house, you can use a 15-ounce can of good-quality diced tomatoes.

EXCHANGES/CHOICES
2 Starch
1 Vegetable
4 Protein, lean

CALORIES 355 | CALORIES FROM FAT 55
TOTAL FAT 6.0 g | SATURATED FAT 0.9 g | TRANS FAT 0.0 g
CHOLESTEROL 35 mg | SODIUM 475 mg | POTASSIUM 1280 mg
TOTAL CARBOHYDRATE 36 g | DIETARY FIBER 14 g | SUGARS 3 g
PROTEIN 35 g | PHOSPHORUS 460 mg

venetian shrimp with garlic (schie aglio olio)

SERVES: 8 | SERVING SIZE: 2 OUNCES SHRIMP

This dish is one that is typically served in Venice in the cicchetti bars.

---

1 pound of small shrimp, peeled and deveined

1 large lemon, juiced

2 cloves garlic

1 tablespoon extra virgin olive oil

1 cup chopped fresh parsley

1/4 teaspoon fine sea salt

1 | Bring a 4-quart pot filled with water to a boil. Boil the shrimp until they are pink outside and opaque inside, about 3 minutes. Remove from pot with slotted spoon. Toss with lemon juice, garlic, extra virgin olive oil, parsley, and salt.

2 | Serve with some cooked polenta or top a green salad with this mixture.

EXCHANGES/CHOICES
1 Protein, lean
1/2 Fat

CALORIES 65 | CALORIES FROM FAT 20
TOTAL FAT 2.5 g | SATURATED FAT 0.4 g | TRANS FAT 0.0 g
CHOLESTEROL 75 mg | SODIUM 240 mg | POTASSIUM 110 mg
TOTAL CARBOHYDRATE 2 g | DIETARY FIBER 0 g | SUGARS 0 g
PROTEIN 8 g | PHOSPHORUS 115 mg

VENETIAN SHRIMP WITH GARLIC (SCHIE AGLIO OLIO)

how to
PEEL AND DEVEIN SHRIMP

To purchase fresh shrimp, make sure it smells like the sea and is not sticky. I often purchase my shrimp frozen and defrost it myself at home because most shrimp are frozen until they arrive at the store anyway.

1   Begin by peeling the shell from the top of the shrimp all the way to the tail.

2   Using a paring knife, cut along the back of the shrimp exposing the vein.

3   Once the vein is exposed, pull out the vein with your paring knife.

balsamic salmon on a bed of barley pilaf
with tomato and basil

SERVES: 4 | SERVING SIZE: 4 OUNCES SALMON, 1 CUP BARLEY, AND 1 CUP VEGETABLES

This recipe works with other thick fillets as well. For instance, if you feel you'd like a change from salmon, try it with cod or halibut

---

1 tablespoon canola oil

1 medium onion, finely chopped

1 large clove garlic, finely minced

2 stalks celery, thinly sliced (about 2 cups)

4 carrots, thinly sliced (about 1 1/2 cups)

1 cup barley, uncooked

3 cups low-sodium chicken stock

1 pint cherry tomatoes, cut in half

1/4 cup balsamic vinegar

1/2 cup basil leaves, roughly chopped

1/4 teaspoon fine sea salt

1/8 teaspoon freshly ground black pepper

1 pound salmon fillet, skin removed, cut into 4 pieces

1 | Place canola oil in large stockpot. Heat and add onion, garlic, and celery. Cook over medium heat, covered, until onion becomes translucent. Add carrots and barley and cook uncovered until barley begins to look toasted. Add stock. Cover and cook 30 minutes.

2 | Slice tomatoes in half and place in large bowl with balsamic vinegar, basil, salt, pepper, and salmon. Let this sit while the barley is cooking for the first 30 minutes. After 30 minutes, remove salmon from tomato mixture. Stir tomato mixture into barley and place salmon on top of barley. Cover and cook 10 minutes more to steam the salmon.

3 | Place some barley pilaf in a pasta bowl and top with a piece of salmon.

EXCHANGES/CHOICES
2 1/2 Starch
3 Vegetable
3 Protein, lean
1 Fat

CALORIES 455 | CALORIES FROM FAT 110
TOTAL FAT 12.0 g | SATURATED FAT 2.1 g | TRANS FAT 0.0 g
CHOLESTEROL 55 mg | SODIUM 315 mg | POTASSIUM 1305 mg
TOTAL CARBOHYDRATE 53 g | DIETARY FIBER 12 g | SUGARS 10 g
PROTEIN 35 g | PHOSPHORUS 485 mg

lemon garlic shrimp on a cucumber flower

SERVES: 12 | SERVING SIZE: 2 PIECES

To cut down on carbs at happy hour, you can use veggies in place of crackers or bread. This recipe not only does that, but it looks beautiful as well!

---

1 pound medium shrimp, peeled and deveined

1 lemon, juiced

2 cloves garlic, crushed and minced to a paste (see How to Make Garlic Paste, page 65)

2 tablespoons extra virgin olive oil

1/2 cup chopped dill

1/4 teaspoon fine sea salt

1/8 teaspoon freshly ground pepper

1 large English cucumber (enough to make 24 slices)

Dill sprigs for garnish

1 | Steam shrimp in large pot with steamer basket insert. Cook just until pink, about 5–6 minutes.

2 | Mix lemon juice, garlic, olive oil, chopped dill, salt, and pepper. Marinate shrimp in this mixture for at least 1 hour and up to 24 hours.

3 | Scrub cucumber well. Take a fork and run it up and down the outside of cucumber to make a decorative edge. Slice cucumber into 24 rounds.

4 | Place one piece of shrimp on a cucumber slice and garnish with another sprig of fresh dill. Cover and refrigerate until serving time.

EXCHANGES/CHOICES
1 Protein, lean

CALORIES 55 | CALORIES FROM FAT 20
TOTAL FAT 2.5 g | SATURATED FAT 0.4 g | TRANS FAT 0.0 g
CHOLESTEROL 50 mg | SODIUM 155 mg | POTASSIUM 85 mg
TOTAL CARBOHYDRATE 2 g | DIETARY FIBER 0 g | SUGARS 1 g
PROTEIN 6 g | PHOSPHORUS 80 mg

how to
STEAM SHRIMP

1   Peel and devein shrimp (see page 80).

3   Place shrimp in basket.

5   Steam until the shrimp turn pink, about 5–6 minutes.

4   Cover pot with lid.

2   Place steamer basket in large pot.

southwestern couscous salad

SERVES: 8 | SERVING SIZE: 1 CUP

Large grain couscous adds texture to your dishes but it does take longer to cook than regular couscous. This pairs well with the Basic Grilled Chicken recipe (page 127).

2 cups couscous (large preferred, but small will work)

4–5 cups chicken or vegetable broth

2 ears fresh corn, steamed until tender

15 ounces black beans, drained and rinsed well

1 red bell pepper, diced same size as beans

1 medium onion, diced same size as beans

4 plum tomatoes chopped

1/4 cup freshly squeezed lime juice

1–2 teaspoons ground cumin

1–2 pinches fine sea salt

1/2 teaspoon freshly ground black pepper

2 cloves garlic, minced

1 tablespoon fresh oregano, chopped

1/4 cup extra virgin olive oil

Fresh cilantro for garnish

Basic Grilled Chicken (page 127)

1 | Cook couscous according to package directions, using broth instead of water.

2 | Mix couscous and vegetables.

3 | Place lime juice in large bowl. Add cumin, salt, pepper, garlic, and oregano. Slowly whisk in olive oil. Add to vegetables and toss well. Taste and adjust seasonings to your liking.

4 | Place a scoop of couscous salad on a dinner plate and set a piece of grilled chicken askew. Garnish with fresh herbs and chopped tomatoes.

Chef's Secret

Great for picnics, make-ahead meals, or brown bag lunches.

EXCHANGES/CHOICES
3 Starch
1 Vegetable
1 Fat

CALORIES 295 | CALORIES FROM FAT 70
TOTAL FAT 8.0 g | SATURATED FAT 1.1 g | TRANS FAT 0.0 g
CHOLESTEROL 0 mg | SODIUM 560 mg | POTASSIUM 440 mg
TOTAL CARBOHYDRATE 47 g | DIETARY FIBER 6 g | SUGARS 5 g
PROTEIN 10 g | PHOSPHORUS 160 mg

how to
CHOP A BELL PEPPER

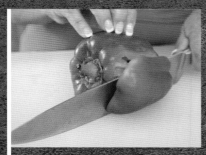

1   Place the pepper on a cutting surface. Imagine that it has four sides and slice off side 1.

2   Repeat with the remaining 3 sides.

3   You can then julienne or chop as needed.

how to
SEPARATE EGGS

1   Crack the egg on a flat surface.

2   Using the shell, pass the egg back and forth between the shells...

3   ... until the white separates from the yolk.

zucchini and canadian bacon omelet

SERVES: 1 | SERVING SIZE: 1 OMELET

One of the ways you can cut down on saturated fat and cholesterol is to substitute 2 egg whites for each whole egg called for in a recipe.

---

1 ounce fully cooked Canadian bacon

1/2 cup diced zucchini

1 whole egg

2 egg whites

Nonstick cooking spray

1 | Spray a large sauté pan with the nonstick cooking spray. Add Canadian bacon and zucchini and cook until brown.

2 | Whisk egg and egg whites in a separate bowl. Add Canadian bacon and zucchini mixture. Scramble until set.

3 | Serve and season as desired.

Serving Suggestion

Garnish with fresh herbs or a light sprinkling of Parmigiano-Reggiano cheese.

EXCHANGES/CHOICES
3 Protein, lean

CALORIES 140 | CALORIES FROM FAT 55
TOTAL FAT 6.0 g | SATURATED FAT 2.0 g | TRANS FAT 0.0 g
CHOLESTEROL 195 mg | SODIUM 405 mg | POTASSIUM 395 mg
TOTAL CARBOHYDRATE 3 g | DIETARY FIBER 1 g | SUGARS 2 g
PROTEIN 18 g | PHOSPHORUS 175 mg

chicken cacciatore

SERVES: 4 | SERVING SIZE: 4 OUNCES CHICKEN AND 1/2 CUP PASTA

Chicken Cacciatore translates to "chicken in the hunter's style." The story behind the name is that if the hunter came home without a catch, the wife could always prepare a chicken. You can easily prepare this dish in a skillet on top of the stove or start it in the skillet and transfer to the oven or slow cooker to finish cooking.

---

2 teaspoons Stress Free Cooking Italian Seasoning Blend (page 9)

1 pound boneless, skinless chicken thighs (four, 4-ounce pieces of chicken)

2 tablespoons extra virgin olive oil

2 cups sliced mushrooms, preferably baby bella or cremini

1 bell pepper, seeded and sliced thinly

1/2 cup chopped onion (about 1 small onion)

2 large cloves garlic, chopped

1 cup sliced celery, about 2 stalks

2 cups crushed tomatoes with basil

1/2 cup dry red wine, such as Sangiovese or Chianti

1/2 pound whole-grain angel hair pasta (I used Barilla Plus), cooked according to package directions

1 | Sprinkle the Stress Free Cooking Italian Seasoning Blend over the chicken thighs.

2 | Place the olive oil in large skillet. Heat oil and add chicken. Brown chicken on first side, turn, and brown on second side. While chicken is browning, add mushrooms, bell pepper, onion, garlic, and celery to pan. Once chicken is browned on both sides, add tomatoes and wine. Bring to a boil and immediately turn to low or simmer, just below a boil.

3 | Cover and cook for 30 minutes, or longer if desired. Chicken can also be placed in a 300°F oven at this point.

4 | Serve over angel hair pasta.

EXCHANGES/CHOICES
3 Starch
3 Vegetable
2 Protein, lean
1 1/2 Fat

CALORIES 475 | CALORIES FROM FAT 125
TOTAL FAT 14.0 g | SATURATED FAT 2.9 g | TRANS FAT 0.0 g
CHOLESTEROL 105 mg | SODIUM 445 mg | POTASSIUM 1005 mg
TOTAL CARBOHYDRATE 59 g | DIETARY FIBER 11 g | SUGARS 10 g
PROTEIN 31 g | PHOSPHORUS 420 mg

spicy garlic ginger chicken

SERVES: 4 | SERVING SIZE: 1 1/2 CUPS

This quick, easy, no fuss dish is hot, spicy, and full of bold flavor. You can adjust the spicy heat by varying the amount of hot chili sauce.

---

2 tablespoons canola oil

2 inches fresh ginger, peeled and minced

2 large cloves garlic, peeled and sliced

16 ounces boneless, skinless chicken breast, sliced for stir-fry

16 ounces baby bok choy, washed and quartered

1 red bell pepper, seeded and thinly sliced

1 cup sliced scallion

1 cup lower-sodium stock, vegetable or chicken

2 teaspoons low-sodium soy sauce

2 teaspoons hot chili sauce

2/3 cup chopped fresh cilantro

2 cups cooked brown rice

1 | Place canola oil in wok or large sauté pan. Add ginger and cook until fragrant. Add garlic and chicken and stir-fry until chicken is no longer translucent.

2 | Add bok choy, bell pepper, and scallion and cook until bok choy begins to wilt.

3 | Add stock, soy sauce, chili sauce and cilantro. Stir-fry until hot and well blended. Serve over brown rice.

EXCHANGES/CHOICES
1 1/2 Starch
2 Vegetable
3 Protein, lean
1 Fat

CALORIES 345 | CALORIES FROM FAT 100
TOTAL FAT 11.0 g | SATURATED FAT 1.5 g | TRANS FAT 0.0 g
CHOLESTEROL 65 mg | SODIUM 320 mg | POTASSIUM 760 mg
TOTAL CARBOHYDRATE 32 g | DIETARY FIBER 5 g | SUGARS 5 g
PROTEIN 30 g | PHOSPHORUS 345 mg

SPICY GARLIC GINGER CHICKEN

how to STIR-FRY

- Make sure all knives are sharp

- Do all prep (cleaning, chopping) in advance, cut longer cooking vegetables into smaller pieces than quicker cooking items.

- Partially freeze meats to make slicing easier

- Marinate meat, chicken, or fish. Fish: 20 minutes, chicken: 20 mins to 1 hour, meat: 1–2 hours.

- Assemble all ingredients *mise en place* (ahead of time).

- Heat wok or large sauté pan prior to adding oil and food.

- Add oil.

- Add foods in order of cooking time—slow cooking first, then quick cooking. Cook vegetables first, remove and then cook meat or fish.

- Add seasonings and combine meat, fish, and vegetables.

- Sauces can be thickened by adding a mixture of liquid thickened with cornstarch. Basic recipe: 1 teaspoon cornstarch dissolved in 1/4 cup water or stock. Cook until sauce is thickened and clear.

SIGNATURE SKILLET SUPPER

signature skillet supper

SERVES: 6 | SERVING SIZE: 1 1/2 CUPS

I love creating versatile recipes that you can tailor to your family's preferences. Use this basic concept and vary the veggies and seasoning for a different taste each time you make this dish. This is also great because it's a one-pot dish. I also recommend trying it with ground turkey or ground buffalo, which has almost no saturated fat.

---

1 tablespoon extra virgin olive oil

1 pound lean ground beef
 (I used 93% lean)

1 cup chopped onion

2 cloves garlic, minced

4 cups frozen mixed vegetables

2 teaspoons togarashi
 (Japanese pepper blend)

3 cups uncooked no yolk
 medium noodles

4 cups low-sodium beef broth

1–2 cups water

1 | Place olive oil in large sauté pan or skillet. Add beef, onions, and garlic and cook until beef is browned. Add vegetables and the seasoning, and mix well. Add the noodles and mix well. Add the broth and enough water to cover everything.

2 | Bring to a boil. Reduce heat to medium and cook until noodles are tender, approximately 15 minutes.

Chef's Secret

Togarashi is a Japanese pepper blend. You can find it in Asian markets or online, or you can substitute any of your favorite mixed pepper blends.

EXCHANGES/CHOICES
1 1/2 Starch
1 Vegetable
2 Protein, lean
1 Fat

CALORIES 285 | **CALORIES FROM FAT** 70
TOTAL FAT 8.0 g | **SATURATED FAT** 2.8 g | **TRANS FAT** 0.4 g
CHOLESTEROL 50 mg | **SODIUM** 165 mg | **POTASSIUM** 590 mg
TOTAL CARBOHYDRATE 28 g | **DIETARY FIBER** 6.g | **SUGARS** 5 g
PROTEIN 23 g | **PHOSPHORUS** 260 mg

part 5
IN THE OVEN

Cooking in the oven is convenient and can be tailored to your needs by varying time and temperature. For instance, when my children had afterschool activities, I would put dinner in the oven and adjust the temperature so that it took a little longer to cook and then dinner would be ready when we arrived at home after the game. It is also a great way to reheat items that you have cooked ahead. Completely covering the food will prevent it from drying out.

There are ovens that have traditional settings as well as convection ovens. Convection ovens have a circulating fan that helps maintain a more even, constant temperature. Convection ovens also cook your food more quickly than traditional or regular settings. A general guideline is that you can expect the cooking time to be reduced by approximately 25% and the temperature can also be reduced by 25°F. Baking can be done in either convection or traditional ovens.

Roasting is a dry heat method of cooking. The meat or veggies are seasoned and placed in an open pan in your oven until they are cooked through. An instant-read meat thermometer is exceptionally helpful when roasting. It is placed in the protein in the coldest part or the center of the product and a temperature is obtained to determine proper doneness.

Braising can be done in your oven or on the stovetop. I prefer braising in the oven so that my heat is even and temperature is more controlled. Braising is cooking slowly in liquid for longer periods of time so that the protein becomes very tender. In this book you will find recipes for several braised dishes. These recipes can also be cooked in the crockpot.

eggplant caviar

SERVES: 12 | SERVING SIZE: 2 TABLESPOONS

When entertaining, it's a great idea to have some healthy dips and spreads in your repertoire and this simple, elegant dish certainly fits the bill.

1 medium eggplant, about 1 1/2 pounds

1 teaspoon extra virgin olive oil

2 shallots, finely minced

2 tablespoons finely chopped Italian parsley

1/4 teaspoon fine sea salt

1/4 teaspoon freshly ground black pepper

1 | Preheat oven to 425°F.

2 | Cut eggplant in half lengthwise. Sprinkle olive oil over both halves. Place on parchment-lined baking sheet, cut side up.

3 | Bake until very soft, about 30 minutes.

4 | Using a fork, pull flesh from eggplant skin and place in mixing bowl. Add remaining ingredients and mix well.

5 | Can be made ahead and refrigerated. Serve either at room temperature or chilled.

EXCHANGES/CHOICES
1 Vegetable

CALORIES 20 | CALORIES FROM FAT 0
TOTAL FAT 0.0 g | SATURATED FAT 0.1 g | TRANS FAT 0.0 g
CHOLESTEROL 0 mg | SODIUM 45 mg | POTASSIUM 70 mg
TOTAL CARBOHYDRATE 5 g | DIETARY FIBER 1 g | SUGARS 2 g
PROTEIN 0 g | PHOSPHORUS 10 mg

roasted eggplant with tomato and basil

SERVES: 2 | SERVING SIZE: 1/2 EGGPLANT

1 medium eggplant, about 1 1/2 pounds

1 teaspoon extra virgin olive oil

1 pint cherry or grape tomatoes, quartered

1/2 cup basil leaves, torn

1/4 teaspoon fine sea salt

1/4 teaspoon freshly ground black pepper

1 tablespoon extra virgin olive oil

1 tablespoon balsamic vinegar

1 | Preheat oven to 425°F.

2 | Cut eggplant in half lengthwise. Sprinkle the teaspoon of olive oil over both halves and rub evenly on cut surface. Place on parchment-lined baking sheet, cut side up. Bake until very soft, about 30 minutes.

3 | In the meantime, prepare the tomato-basil mixture. Place tomatoes, basil, salt, pepper, the remaining olive oil, and vinegar in a bowl and mix well.

4 | Once the eggplant is roasted, spoon the tomato-basil mixture over each piece of eggplant. The heat from the eggplant will warm the tomato mixture and the basil will become very fragrant.

EXCHANGES/CHOICES
7 Vegetable
1 1/2 Fat

CALORIES 225 | CALORIES FROM FAT 90
TOTAL FAT 10.0 g | SATURATED FAT 1.4 g | TRANS FAT 0.0 g
CHOLESTEROL 0 mg | SODIUM 285 mg | POTASSIUM 795 mg
TOTAL CARBOHYDRATE 35 g | DIETARY FIBER 10 g | SUGARS 15 g
PROTEIN 4 g | PHOSPHORUS 90 mg

zucchini mushroom quiche

SERVES: 8 | SERVING SIZE: 1 SLICE

I love using Italian pancetta as a substitute for bacon. It is full of flavor and much less fatty than American-style bacon. Crustless quiche is one way to cut back on fat and calories since pie crust is very high in fat.

Nonstick olive oil cooking spray

1 ounce pancetta, cut into 1/4-inch dice

1/2 cup diced zucchini

1/2 cup sliced cremini mushrooms

2 cups egg substitute

1 cup fat-free half & half

1/2 teaspoon fine sea salt

1/4 teaspoon freshly ground black pepper

1 cup shredded low-fat cheese such as Italian blend

1 | Spray a large skillet with nonstick olive oil spray. Saute pancetta until golden brown. Add the zucchini and mushrooms and sauté until wilted.

2 | Whisk the eggs and half and half in a mixing bowl. Season with salt and pepper.

3 | Place the pancetta veggie mixture in 9-inch pie plate or quiche pan that has been sprayed with nonstick cooking spray. Pour the egg mixture over. Top with the cheese.

4 | Bake at 375°F for 30 minutes until golden and set in the center. Cut into 8 slices.

EXCHANGES/CHOICES
1/2 Carbohydrate
1 Protein, lean

CALORIES 90 | CALORIES FROM FAT 25
TOTAL FAT 3.0 g | SATURATED FAT 1.5 g | TRANS FAT 0.0 g
CHOLESTEROL 10 mg | SODIUM 425 mg | POTASSIUM 215 mg
TOTAL CARBOHYDRATE 5 g | DIETARY FIBER 0 g | SUGARS 2 g
PROTEIN 10 g | PHOSPHORUS 125 mg

ZUCCHINI MUSHROOM QUICHE

CRUNCHY QUINOA STUFFED ZUCCHINI

crunchy quinoa stuffed zucchini

SERVES: 6 | SERVING SIZE: 1/2 ZUCCHINI

This is a great way to add more grains to your diet and the quinoa gets a wonderful crunch when baked.

1/2 cup uncooked quinoa, rinsed

3 zucchini, each weighing about 1/2 pound

1 teaspoon extra virgin olive oil

2 ounces chopped pancetta

3/4 cup chopped onion (about 1 medium)

1 large clove garlic, minced

3/4 cup halved cherry or grape tomatoes, quartered if large

Chef's Secret

The quinoa mixture is also great when used as a side dish.

---

1 | Preheat oven to 425°F convection or 450°F traditional oven.

2 | Place quinoa in medium saucepan with 1 cup water. Bring to a boil, reduce heat to low, cover, and cook 15–20 minutes until tender.

3 | Cut zucchini in half lengthwise. Using a paring knife, cut a V shape into each half and remove the center, creating a channel for the stuffing. Chop the zucchini that has been removed and save it for use in the stuffing.

4 | In the meantime, place the olive oil in a large sauté pan. Add pancetta, onion, garlic, and chopped zucchini. Sauté until pancetta is browned. Remove pan from heat and add tomatoes. Add cooked quinoa and mix well.

5 | Stuff each zucchini half with 1/2 cup quinoa mixture and place on parchment-lined baking sheet.

6 | Bake 20–25 minutes until zucchini are fork tender. Stuffing will be nicely browned.

EXCHANGES/CHOICES
1/2 Starch
1 Vegetable
1 Fat

CALORIES 125 | **CALORIES FROM FAT** 45
TOTAL FAT 5.0 g | **SATURATED FAT** 1.3 g | **TRANS FAT** 0.0 g
CHOLESTEROL 10 mg | **SODIUM** 190 mg | **POTASSIUM** 485 mg
TOTAL CARBOHYDRATE 17 g | **DIETARY FIBER** 3 g | **SUGARS** 4 g
PROTEIN 5 g | **PHOSPHORUS** 170 mg

oven roasted potatoes with rosemary and garlic

SERVES: 6 | SERVING SIZE: 1/2 CUP

---

3 pounds potatoes such as Yukon gold or red bliss

2 tablespoons fresh rosemary

8 garlic cloves, whole, peeled

1 tablespoon extra virgin olive oil

1 teaspoon fine sea salt

1/2 teaspoon freshly ground pepper or more, if desired

1 | Preheat oven to 425°F.

2 | Wash and dry potatoes. Cut into bite-size pieces unless you are using baby potatoes.

3 | Strip rosemary from stems. Slightly bruise with chef's knife. Peel garlic.

4 | Place potatoes, rosemary, and garlic in large mixing bowl. Add olive oil to evenly coat potatoes. Sprinkle with salt and pepper.

5 | Place on parchment-lined baking sheet in single layer.

6 | Roast in oven 30 minutes to 1 hour, depending on size of potato, or until fork tender and golden brown.

Chef's Secret

Tossing the potatoes with the oil in a large bowl as opposed to drizzling the baking sheet with extra virgin olive oil will require less oil.

EXCHANGES/CHOICES
2 1/2 Starch

CALORIES 185 | CALORIES FROM FAT 20
TOTAL FAT 2.5 g | SATURATED FAT 0.4 g | TRANS FAT 0.0 g
CHOLESTEROL 0 mg | SODIUM 375 mg | POTASSIUM 895 mg
TOTAL CARBOHYDRATE 38 g | DIETARY FIBER 5 g | SUGARS 2 g
PROTEIN 4 g | PHOSPHORUS 125 mg

roasted root vegetables with garlic

SERVES: 12 | SERVING SIZE: 1/2 CUP

This is a great way to incorporate the less common veggies such as parsnips and turnips into our diet. Roasting makes any veggie taste great!

3 turnips, scrubbed or peeled,
  cut into 1-inch chunks

3 carrots, scrubbed or peeled,
  cut into 1-inch chunks

3 Yukon gold potatoes, scrubbed,
  unpeeled, and cut into 1-inch chunks

3 parsnips, scrubbed or peeled,
  cut into 1-inch chunks

8 shallots, peeled

1 head garlic, cloves separated
  and peeled

1 teaspoon fine sea salt

1 teaspoon freshly ground pepper

2 tablespoons extra virgin olive oil

Good-quality balsamic vinegar
  (optional)

Fresh herb sprigs for garnish

1 | Preheat oven to 425°F.

2 | Place all veggies in large bowl and toss with olive oil, salt, and pepper.

3 | Line baking sheet with parchment. Place vegetables on baking sheet. Roast to desired doneness, approximately 40–45 minutes.

4 | Taste to adjust seasonings. Place on serving platter and sprinkle with balsamic vinegar. Garnish with fresh herbs.

EXCHANGES/CHOICES
1 Starch
1 Vegetable

CALORIES 105 | **CALORIES FROM FAT** 20
TOTAL FAT 2.5 g | **SATURATED FAT** 0.4 g | **TRANS FAT** 0.0 g
CHOLESTEROL 0 mg | **SODIUM** 220 mg | **POTASSIUM** 470 mg
TOTAL CARBOHYDRATE 20 g | **DIETARY FIBER** 4 g | **SUGARS** 4 g
PROTEIN 2 g | **PHOSPHORUS** 70 mg

roasted vegetables

SERVES: 12 | SERVING SIZE: 1/2 CUP

All veggies are delicious when roasted. Their flavors are enhanced and the natural sugars are caramelized, giving a nice crunch. Vary this recipe by using whatever veggies you like or roast one single vegetable at a time.

---

1 small eggplant, unpeeled, cut into 1-inch chunks (whatever color you like)

1 zucchini, sliced into 1-inch pieces

1 yellow squash, sliced into 1-inch pieces

10 ounces cremini mushrooms

4 shallots, peeled and quartered

1 red bell pepper, cut into 1-inch chunks

1 green bell pepper, cut into 1-inch chunks

1 yellow bell pepper, cut into 1-inch chunks

1 head garlic, cloves separated and peeled

2 tablespoons extra virgin olive oil

1 teaspoon fine sea salt

1 teaspoon freshly ground pepper

Good-quality balsamic vinegar

Fresh herb sprigs for garnish

1 | Preheat oven to 425°F.

2 | Place eggplant in bowl large enough to hold all of the veggies. Lightly salt eggplant and let sit for 10 minutes. This will prevent it from absorbing too much oil. Add remaining vegetables and toss with olive oil.

3 | Line baking sheet with parchment. Place vegetables on baking sheet. Sprinkle with salt and pepper to taste.

4 | Roast to desired doneness, approximately 20–30 minutes. Taste to adjust seasonings. Place on serving platter and sprinkle with balsamic vinegar. Garnish with fresh herbs.

Chef's Secret

One of the tricks to roasting veggies is to make sure that you consider texture when cutting them. Cut harder veggies like carrots or potatoes into smaller pieces than the softer eggplant or zucchini if you are roasting them together.

Serving Suggestion

Toss with whole-grain pasta and serve at room temperature with a dressing of extra virgin olive oil and balsamic vinegar.

EXCHANGES/CHOICES
1 Vegetable
1/2 Fat

CALORIES 60 | CALORIES FROM FAT 20
TOTAL FAT 2.5 g | SATURATED FAT 0.4 g | TRANS FAT 0.0 g
CHOLESTEROL 0 mg | SODIUM 185 mg | POTASSIUM 345 mg
TOTAL CARBOHYDRATE 9 g | DIETARY FIBER 2 g | SUGARS 4 g
PROTEIN 2 g | PHOSPHORUS 65 mg

roasted garlic

SERVES: 6 | SERVING SIZE: 1 TABLESPOON

Roasted garlic is great to have on hand to add rich flavor to sauces and dressings. It is also great as a bruschetta topping.

---

4 large heads of garlic

1 teaspoon extra virgin olive oil

1/2 teaspoon fine sea salt

Freshly ground pepper

1 | Preheat oven to 400°F.

2 | Using a chef's knife, slice a thin piece off the top or stem end of the garlic to expose most of the cloves.

3 | Place heads on large sheet of aluminum foil and drizzle with just enough olive oil to moisten the garlic, approximately 1/4 teaspoon per head. This will vary depending on the size of the garlic. Sprinkle with a dash of sea salt and freshly ground pepper.

4 | Wrap garlic tightly and place in ceramic dish. Bake approximately 45 minutes or until very soft to the touch and a spreadable consistency. Let cool and then squeeze from skins and mash to a puréed consistency. Refrigerate and use as needed.

Variations

Break cloves apart, drizzle with oil, season with salt and pepper, and roast in foil 20–30 minutes. Peel garlic cloves, drizzle with oil, season with salt and pepper, and roast in foil 20 minutes.

EXCHANGES/CHOICES
1 Carbohydrate

CALORIES 60 | CALORIES FROM FAT 10
TOTAL FAT 1.0 g | SATURATED FAT 0.1 g | TRANS FAT 0.0 g
CHOLESTEROL 0 mg | SODIUM 185 mg | POTASSIUM 145 mg
TOTAL CARBOHYDRATE 12 g | DIETARY FIBER 1 g | SUGARS 0 g
PROTEIN 2 g | PHOSPHORUS 55 mg

STUFFED ARTICHOKES

stuffed artichokes

SERVES: 12 | SERVING SIZE: 1/2 MEDIUM ARTICHOKE

I don't think I've ever met anyone who doesn't love a stuffed artichoke! Since they come in different sizes, you can always halve them after baking if they are too large.

---

2 lemons

Large bowl of water

6 fresh medium artichokes

STUFFING

1/4 pound pancetta, finely diced

1 clove garlic, finely minced

1/4 cup toasted pignoli (pine) nuts, chopped

1 cup fresh breadcrumbs

3 tablespoons freshly grated Parmigiano-Reggiano cheese

1/4 cup minced fresh parley

2 pinches fine sea salt

Few grinds freshly ground black pepper

1 | Squeeze lemons into bowl of water to keep artichokes from browning while cleaning them.

2 | Clean artichokes. Cut stems from artichokes, peel off any outer leaves, and trim remaining leaves.

3 | Place each artichoke in the acidulated water while cleaning remaining artichokes.

4 | Place artichokes right side up in Dutch oven or covered saucepan and fill pan with water to come halfway up the side of artichokes. Cook approximately 40 minutes until artichokes are tender and leaves are removed easily.

5 | Remove from pan, drain, and cool until you can handle. While artichokes are cooling, prepare stuffing.

6 | Preheat oven to 400°F. Place pancetta in large sauté pan. Cook until crisp. Add garlic and nuts. Cook until garlic is fragrant. Add breadcrumbs, parsley, salt, and pepper. Cool and add cheese.

7 | Gently pull/separate artichoke leaves and remove choke (fuzzy bottom). (A grapefruit spoon works well.)

8 | Stuff each artichoke with this mixture and place stuffed artichokes in baking dish. Bake until golden, approximately 20 minutes.

EXCHANGES/CHOICES
1/2 Carbohydrate
1 Fat

CALORIES 100 | CALORIES FROM FAT 55
TOTAL FAT 6.0 g | SATURATED FAT 1.5 g | TRANS FAT 0.0 g
CHOLESTEROL 10 mg | SODIUM 260 mg | POTASSIUM 225 mg
TOTAL CARBOHYDRATE 9 g | DIETARY FIBER 5 g | SUGARS 1 g
PROTEIN 4 g | PHOSPHORUS 110 mg

stress free vertical chicken

SERVES: 8 | SERVING SIZE: 2 DRUMSTICKS, 2 THIGHS, 2 WINGS WITH SOME BREAST MEAT, OR 2 BREAST HALVES

This recipe uses a vertical chicken roaster. This method of cooking sears the chicken inside and out while any fat drips from the chicken. The chicken browns beautifully all around.

---

1 whole roasting chicken, about 3 pounds

1/4 cup Stress Free Cooking Seasoning Blend (page 9) or Stress Free Cooking Italian Seasoning Blend (page 9)

Nonstick cooking spray

1 | Preheat oven to 375°F.

2 | Spray the vertical chicken roaster and a roasting pan or baking dish with nonstick cooking spray.

3 | Sprinkle the chicken all around with the Stress Free Cooking Seasoning Blend of your choice. Place the chicken on the vertical roaster and place the roaster in a roasting pan or oven-safe baking dish.

4 | Place in the oven and bake 1 hour until golden brown and internal temperature reaches 165°F.

5 | Cut chicken into 8 servings: 2 legs, 2 wings, 2 thighs, and 2 breast halves. Remove skin before serving.

EXCHANGES/CHOICES
2 Protein, lean

CALORIES 105 | **CALORIES FROM FAT** 35
TOTAL FAT 4.0 g | **SATURATED FAT** 1.1 g | **TRANS FAT** 0.0 g
CHOLESTEROL 50 mg | **SODIUM** 210 mg | **POTASSIUM** 140 mg
TOTAL CARBOHYDRATE 0 g | **DIETARY FIBER** 0 g | **SUGARS** 0 g
PROTEIN 16 g | **PHOSPHORUS** 110 mg

how to
COOK IN PARCHMENT

Cooking in parchment is a great way to cut down on added fats in your recipes. The parchment paper serves as a nonstick medium. It is also great when used to line all your baking or roasting pans in place of butter or oils. The instructions are specific to the preparation of the Chicken and Vegetables en Papillote recipe (page 108), but cooking any dish in parchment is a similar process.

1   Fold the parchment in half. Cut into a heart shape.

3   Place the potato and chicken breast on one half of the heart.

5   Fold the other half of the heart over and begin crimping the edges.

2   Slice a potato about 1/8-inch thick.

6   Finish with a tightly sealed package that will go on a baking sheet.

4   Top the chicken with the julienned vegetables and chopped garlic. Drizzle with dry white wine.

chicken and vegetables en papillote

SERVES: 4 | SERVING SIZE: 1 PACKAGE

This is a dramatic dish to serve to guests. When you place the parchment package on each guest's dinner plate, the steam and the flavors are intoxicating! Fish fillets also work well in this recipe.

Parchment paper

24 thin slices of Yukon gold potatoes
 (about 1 small potato per person)

4 pieces boneless, skinless chicken breast
 (approximately 4 ounces each)

4 cloves garlic, minced

4 sprigs rosemary

4 sprigs thyme

24 fresh green beans

12 baby carrots, halved lengthwise

1 small yellow squash, cut into 16
 julienned pieces

1 teaspoon Stress Free Cooking Seasoning
 Blend (page 9)

1/2 cup dry white wine, such as Pinot
 Grigio, Soave, Orvieto, or Sauvignon Blanc

1 | Preheat oven to 375°F.

2 | Cut four sheets of parchment (about 18 inches long) and then fold each in half lengthwise. Cut each in a 1/2 heart shape, which will make a heart when fully open.

3 | Working on 1/2 of the heart, layer as follows: potatoes, chicken breast, garlic, rosemary, and thyme, 6 green beans, 4 pieces carrot, and 4 pieces yellow squash. Sprinkle with Stress Free Cooking Seasoning Blend and wine.

4 | Fold the parchment in half and crimp edges all the way around to seal tightly. Place on baking sheet and place in the preheated oven. Bake 25–30 minutes.

Variation

Foil can be used in place of parchment paper and can be cooked outside on the grill.

EXCHANGES/CHOICES
1 1/2 Starch
1 Vegetable
3 Protein, lean

CALORIES 270 | CALORIES FROM FAT 25
TOTAL FAT 3.0 g | SATURATED FAT 0.9 g | TRANS FAT 0.0 g
CHOLESTEROL 65 mg | SODIUM 475 mg | POTASSIUM 895 mg
TOTAL CARBOHYDRATE 30 g | DIETARY FIBER 5 g | SUGARS 4 g
PROTEIN 28 g | PHOSPHORUS 270 mg

OVEN FRIED CHICKEN

oven fried chicken

SERVES: 8 | SERVING SIZE: 1 THIGH

Not only is this "fried" chicken healthier than traditional fried chicken, but it is easier and less messy to prepare than the traditional version.

---

2 cups Italian-style whole-wheat breadcrumbs

1 large clove garlic

1 tablespoon Stress Free Cooking Italian Seasoning Blend (page 9)

1/2 cup all-purpose flour

2 large eggs, whisked with 1 tablespoon water

4 large egg whites

8 boneless, skinless chicken thighs (about 2 pounds)

1 | Preheat oven to 375°F convection or 400°F traditional oven. Place breadcrumbs, garlic, and Stress Free Cooking Italian Seasoning Blend in food processor. Process until well blended.

2 | Place flour in pie plate. Place eggs and egg whites in a separate pie plate. Place breadcrumb mixture in a third pie plate.

3 | Line a large baking sheet with parchment paper.

4 | Dip chicken in flour and coat on all sides, then in egg, and then in breadcrumbs. Coat evenly. Place on parchment-lined baking sheet. If you have time, refrigerate the chicken for a while before cooking.

5 | Bake chicken for 45 minutes until crispy and nicely browned. Serve with picnic condiments or salads. Can be made ahead and frozen for reheating in a very hot oven. Defrost before reheating.

EXCHANGES/CHOICES
1 Starch
3 Protein, lean
1/2 Fat

CALORIES 240 | CALORIES FROM FAT 70
TOTAL FAT 8.0 g | SATURATED FAT 2.3 g | TRANS FAT 0.0 g
CHOLESTEROL 150 mg | SODIUM 320 mg | POTASSIUM 315 mg
TOTAL CARBOHYDRATE 14 g | DIETARY FIBER 2 g | SUGARS 1 g
PROTEIN 25 g | PHOSPHORUS 245 mg

chicken, pasta, and veggie bake

SERVES: 16 | SERVING SIZE: 1 CUP

This recipe was developed in large quantity so you can have one casserole to eat now and one to freeze. One great way to eat healthy is to plan ahead, so having a healthy meal in the freezer for an exceptionally busy week will help you achieve your healthy lifestyle goal.

1 pound small tubular pasta, such as mini penne or mezze rigatoni

3 tablespoons extra virgin olive oil

2 pounds boneless, skinless chicken breast, trimmed and cut into bite-sized pieces

4 teaspoons Stress Free Cooking Italian Seasoning blend (page 9)

4 cloves garlic, minced

1 1/3 cup carrot, diced

1 1/3 cup celery, diced

1 1/3 cup onion, diced

4 cups sliced zucchini

3 cups low-sodium chicken stock

2 cups canned crushed tomatoes

1 | Bring a large pot of water to a boil. Cook pasta, according to package directions, to al dente stage. Drain and set aside.

2 | Place olive oil in large sauté pan and heat to medium. Mix chicken with Stress Free Cooking Italian Seasoning Blend and add garlic. Place in sauté pan and cook until chicken is lightly browned and cooked through. Remove chicken from sauté pan and add carrots, celery, onions, and zucchini. Sauté until the edges of the onion begin to brown. Add chicken stock and tomatoes. Bring to boil. Return chicken to pan and mix well.

3 | Place half the pasta in each of two 9 × 13-inch baking dishes or foil pans. Add half the chicken mixture to each and mix well.

4 | Cool, cover, and label one for the freezer. To reheat, defrost if possible. Defrost by placing in the refrigerator the night before cooking.

5 | Bake the other at 375°F for 30 minutes or until bubbly.

Chef's Secret

2 pounds boneless, skinless chicken breast—cut into bite-sized pieces before cooking—will yield about 4 cups cooked

EXCHANGES/CHOICES
1 1/2 Starch
1 Vegetable
2 Protein, lean

CALORIES 220 | **CALORIES FROM FAT** 40
TOTAL FAT 4.5 g | **SATURATED FAT** 0.9 g | **TRANS FAT** 0.0 g
CHOLESTEROL 35 mg | **SODIUM** 295 mg | **POTASSIUM** 410 mg
TOTAL CARBOHYDRATE 27 g | **DIETARY FIBER** 3 g | **SUGARS** 4 g
PROTEIN 17 g | **PHOSPHORUS** 160 mg

baked scallops with mushroom sauce

SERVES: 4 | SERVING SIZE: 3 OUNCES SCALLOPS, 3 OUNCES SAUCE

The "cream" sauce in this dish is a low-fat, tasty treat!

---

1 tablespoon extra virgin olive oil

1 1/2 pounds mixed mushrooms, roughly chopped

2 tablespoons minced shallots (1 large)

1/2 cup fresh basil, chopped

1/4 cup flat Italian parsley, chopped

1/2 cup dry white wine or chicken stock

1 cup evaporated skim milk

1/4 teaspoon fine sea salt

1/8 teaspoon freshly ground white pepper

12 ounces bay scallops, rinsed

1 | Preheat oven to 400°F.

2 | Heat a large sauté pan and add the olive oil, mushrooms, and shallots. Cook until mushrooms begin to wilt and shallots begin to become translucent, about 3–4 minutes.

3 | Add herbs, wine or stock, evaporated skim milk, salt, and pepper. Bring to boil and immediately turn to low. Add scallops and coat well with sauce. Transfer scallops to ovenproof dish or individual baking dishes. Bake 20 minutes. Serve immediately.

Chef's Secret

Garnish with additional chopped fresh herbs. White pepper is often used in cream sauce so you don't see black pepper specks, but black pepper is okay to use if you don't have white pepper in your pantry.

EXCHANGES/CHOICES
1 Carbohydrate
3 Protein, lean

CALORIES 190 | CALORIES FROM FAT 40
TOTAL FAT 4.5 g | SATURATED FAT 0.7 g | TRANS FAT 0.0 g
CHOLESTEROL 25 mg | SODIUM 580 mg | POTASSIUM 965 mg
TOTAL CARBOHYDRATE 17 g | DIETARY FIBER 2 g | SUGARS 10 g
PROTEIN 21 g | PHOSPHORUS 505 mg

broiled flounder with tropical pineapple slaw

SERVES: 4 | SERVING SIZE: 4 OUNCES FLOUNDER, 1/2 CUP SLAW

1/4 cup light mayonnaise

1/4 teaspoon ground chipotle pepper
(such as McCormick's)

1 (6-ounce) can crushed pineapple

1/2 cup chopped cilantro
(or flat Italian parsley)

2 cups packaged coleslaw mix
(such as Dole or sliced cabbage
from produce section)

Nonstick cooking spray

1 pound flounder fillet

1 | Mix mayonnaise and chipotle pepper together in large bowl. Add pineapple with juice and cilantro. Mix well. Add coleslaw and mix well.

2 | Preheat broiler. Spray foil pan with nonstick cooking spray and place fish in pan. Spray fish with nonstick cooking spray. Place under broiler for 3–5 minutes until fish is flaky.

3 | Serve with tropical slaw. This dish can also be served in a whole-wheat pita.

EXCHANGES/CHOICES
1/2 Carbohydrate
3 Protein, lean

CALORIES 175 | CALORIES FROM FAT 45
TOTAL FAT 5.0 g | SATURATED FAT 0.8 g | TRANS FAT 0.0 g
CHOLESTEROL 65 mg | SODIUM 220 mg | POTASSIUM 440 mg
TOTAL CARBOHYDRATE 9 g | DIETARY FIBER 1 g | SUGARS 6 g
PROTEIN 22 g | PHOSPHORUS 270 mg

eggplant meatballs

SERVES: 15 | SERVING SIZE: 1 MEATBALL

This meatless "meatball" is full of flavor and texture. It's a great alternative to meat.

---

2 pounds fresh eggplant
  (about 10 cups diced)

1 teaspoon fine sea salt

1 tablespoon extra virgin olive oil

2 cups fresh breadcrumbs

3 large eggs

1/2 cup grated Romano cheese

1 tablespoon finely minced garlic

1/2 cup chopped flat Italian parsley

1/2 teaspoon freshly ground black pepper

1 | Preheat oven to 425°F (use convection if you have it).

2 | Wash eggplant and dice into 1/2-inch cubes. Place in large bowl. Sprinkle with the sea salt. Toss well. Let sit 15 minutes. Add olive oil and toss well. Spread on parchment-lined baking sheet and place in preheated oven. Roast 25 minutes or until golden brown. Cool slightly.

3 | Place breadcrumbs, eggs, cheese, garlic, parsley, and black pepper in mixing bowl large enough to hold these ingredients and the roasted eggplant. Mix the breadcrumbs, eggs, cheese, garlic, parsley, and black pepper well. Once the eggplant is golden brown, add it to this mixture and mix well.

4 | Form into 15 "meatballs." Place meatballs on a baking sheet that has been sprayed with nonstick cooking spray. Spread 1 tablespoon of extra virgin olive oil on the baking sheet. Place the meatballs on the baking sheet and turn them in the olive oil to coat.

5 | Bake 25 minutes or until golden. Serve with Quick Fresh Herb Marinara Souce (page 57).

EXCHANGES/CHOICES
1/2 Carbohydrate
1 Fat

CALORIES 75 | CALORIES FROM FAT 35
TOTAL FAT 4.0 g | SATURATED FAT 1.0 g | TRANS FAT 0.0 g
CHOLESTEROL 40 mg | SODIUM 225 mg | POTASSIUM 100 mg
TOTAL CARBOHYDRATE 8 g | DIETARY FIBER 2 g | SUGARS 2 g
PROTEIN 3 g | PHOSPHORUS 55 mg

turkey and sun-dried tomato meatloaf or meatballs

SERVES: 6 | SERVING SIZE: 1 SLICE MEATLOAF

I created this dish as a lighter alternative to beef meatballs and to add variety to our pasta menus. Pair this with the Quick Fresh Herb Marinara Sauce on page 57.

1 1/2 cups dry bread cubes

1 cup dry red wine (Sangiovese or Chianti) or chicken stock

1 pound ground turkey breast

1 cup sun-dried tomatoes (not in oil), cut in bits

1–2 cloves garlic, minced

2 shallots, minced

1/4 cup fresh basil, chopped, or 1 teaspoon dry basil leaves, crushed between your fingers

2 tablespoons fresh oregano, chopped, or 1/2 teaspoon dry oregano, crushed between your fingers

1/4 cup pignoli (pine) nuts, toasted and roughly chopped

1/4 cup freshly grated Parmesan cheese

2 egg whites or 1 whole egg

1 | Preheat oven to 400°F. Soak bread cubes in wine or stock.

2 | Mix all ingredients together in a large bowl. Do not overmix. This will produce a tough meatloaf.

3 | Form into a loaf or meatballs and bake 45 minutes for meatloaf, 20 minutes for meatballs. (Do not use a loaf pan.)

Chef's Secret

Can also be made into individual meatloaves or meatballs and baked 15–20 minutes. Meatballs can also be sautéed until golden.

EXCHANGES/CHOICES
1/2 Starch
1 Vegetable
3 Protein, lean
1/2 Fat

CALORIES 215 | CALORIES FROM FAT 65
TOTAL FAT 7.0 g | SATURATED FAT 1.3 g | TRANS FAT 0.0 g
CHOLESTEROL 45 mg | SODIUM 335 mg | POTASSIUM 645 mg
TOTAL CARBOHYDRATE 14 g | DIETARY FIBER 2 g | SUGARS 5 g
PROTEIN 25 g | PHOSPHORUS 280 mg

chicken caesar meatballs

SERVES: 8 | SERVING SIZE: 2 MEATBALLS

1/2 teaspoon garlic powder

1 large egg

2 tablespoons chopped flat Italian parsley

3 tablespoons freshly grated Parmigiano-Reggiano cheese

1/4 teaspoon fine sea salt

1/4 teaspoon ground black pepper

1/2 cup whole-wheat seasoned breadcrumbs

3 tablespoons freshly squeezed lemon juice (about 1 lemon)

1 pound ground chicken breast

1 | Preheat oven to 375°F (use convection if you have it).

2 | Place all ingredients except the chicken in a large bowl. Mix well and then add the chicken and gently mix. Form into 16 meatballs.

3 | Place on a parchment-lined baking sheet and bake for 20 minutes.

Chef's Secret

You don't want to overmix or your meatballs will be tough. That is why I like to mix everything but the meat together before adding the meat.

EXCHANGES/CHOICES
2 Protein, lean

CALORIES 110 | CALORIES FROM FAT 25
TOTAL FAT 3.0 g | SATURATED FAT 1.1 g | TRANS FAT 0.0 g
CHOLESTEROL 60 mg | SODIUM 245 mg | POTASSIUM 145 mg
TOTAL CARBOHYDRATE 4 g | DIETARY FIBER 0 g | SUGARS 1 g
PROTEIN 16 g | PHOSPHORUS 140 mg

italian-style meatloaf or meatballs

SERVES: 8 | SERVING SIZE: 4 OUNCES

Meatloaf or meatballs seems to be more of an Italian-American dish, but it has certainly become one of our favorite comfort foods. This recipe will make 2 one-pound meatloaves or 20 meatballs. If you are making meatloaves, bake one tonight and freeze the uncooked meatloaf for another night.

---

3 garlic cloves, minced

1 small onion, minced

1/2 cup egg substitute

1 tablespoon chopped fresh basil

1/2 cup chopped fresh parsley

1/4 cup freshly grated Parmesan cheese (optional)

1/2 teaspoon fine sea salt

1/2 teaspoon ground black pepper

1/2 cup Italian-style bread crumbs

1/4 cup low-sodium beef broth or red wine

2 pounds extra-lean (90%) ground beef

1 | Preheat oven to 425°F (or use convection if you have it).

2 | Place all ingredients except the beef in a large bowl. Mix well. Add the beef and gently mix. Form into 2 loaves or roll into 20 meatballs. If the mixture does not hold together, add another 1/4 cup breadcrumbs.

3 | Place on a parchment-lined baking sheet and bake in a very hot oven to brown the outside. It should take about 45 minutes with a convection oven and 60 minutes with a traditional oven.

Chef's Secret

You don't want to overmix or your meatloaf will be tough. That is why I like to the mix everything but the meat together before adding the meat.

EXCHANGES/CHOICES
1/2 Carbohydrate
3 Protein, lean
1 Fat

CALORIES 220 | **CALORIES FROM FAT** 90
TOTAL FAT 10.0 g | **SATURATED FAT** 3.8 g | **TRANS FAT** 0.6 g
CHOLESTEROL 70 mg | **SODIUM** 345 mg | **POTASSIUM** 425 mg
TOTAL CARBOHYDRATE 7 g | **DIETARY FIBER** 1 g | **SUGARS** 1 g
PROTEIN 25 g | **PHOSPHORUS** 215 mg

ITALIAN-STYLE MEATBALLS

mexi-style meatballs

SERVES: 8 | SERVING SIZE: 4 OUNCES

This recipe will make 2 one-pound meatloaves or 20 meatballs. If you are making meatloaves, bake one tonight and freeze the uncooked meatloaf for another night. Serve with Mexi-Style Salad (page 51).

---

1 bunch scallions or green onions, sliced (about 1 cup)

2 cans diced green chilies (about 8 ounces)

2 large eggs

1/2 cup chopped fresh cilantro

1/2 teaspoon fine sea salt

1 teaspoon Hatch chili powder

1/2 cup roasted garlic breadcrumbs

1/2 cup prepared enchilada sauce, plus 1/4 cup for later use

1 pound ground turkey breast

1 pound ground turkey (7% fat)

1 | Preheat oven to 425°F (use convection if you have it).

2 | Place all ingredients except the turkey and 1/4 cup enchilada sauce in a large bowl. Mix well, then add the turkey and gently mix. Form into 2 loaves or roll into 20 meatballs.

3 | Place on a parchment-lined baking sheet and bake for 30 minutes. Spoon the last 1/4 cup enchilada sauce over the meatloaf and bake 5 minutes more.

Chef's Secret

You don't want to overmix or your meatloaf will be tough. I like to mix everything but the meat together first, and then I add the meat and mix lightly.

EXCHANGES/CHOICES
1/2 Carbohydrate
4 Protein, lean

CALORIES 225 | CALORIES FROM FAT 65
TOTAL FAT 7.0 g | SATURATED FAT 2.0 g | TRANS FAT 0.1 g
CHOLESTEROL 120 mg | SODIUM 475 mg | POTASSIUM 500 mg
TOTAL CARBOHYDRATE 9 g | DIETARY FIBER 2 g | SUGARS 2 g
PROTEIN 28 g | PHOSPHORUS 295 mg

part 6
ON THE GRILL

Grilling is a wonderful way to cook! It can be quick, easy, healthy, and requires little or no clean-up. It is also a great casual way to entertain. Many folks commonly confuse "grilling" and barbecuing. Barbecue is a slow cooked piece of meat in a piquant sauce, originating in the South. Grilling is much different.

Weber-Stepen defines grilling as "an art form that depends largely on controlling the fire, getting the seasonings just right, and mastering a special technique." There are many cultures and cuisines that can be explored through grilling. You can visit many of them through the use of different spices, marinades, and rubs. During the summer months, it is especially nice to cook with what's in season.

types of grills

There are many different types of grills. It is not necessary to overbuy. Will you use all those bells and whistles? Grilling can be done indoors or outdoors, at your home, at a picnic ground, or at a tailgate location. Are there any restrictions in your community? The most commonly available grills are:

- GAS GRILLING (outside)—uses lava rocks or flavorizer bars system, sometimes restricted in condo, townhouse, or apartment complexes
- ELECTRIC GRILLING (inside or outside)— one sided or two sided, open or closed
- STOVETOP GRILL PANS (inside)—round, square, single or double burner, with lid or without
- CHARCOAL (outside)—uses charcoal briquettes

recommended grilling tools and accessories

- Spray bottle of water for safety
- Long-handled tools such as tongs, spatulas, etc
- Meat thermometer
- Basting brush—for marinades
- Wire brush for cleaning grill
- Skewers—metal and wooden
- Rotisserie attachment
- Mitts and potholders
- Disposable foil pans

- Grill cover
- Spare tank of propane gas

safety is very important

- Maintain grill properly (see your owner's manual).
- Keep water nearby.
- Do not grill in an area that is not well ventilated.
- Do not grill in extremely windy conditions.
- Drain marinades and sauces from food before placing on the grill to avoid flare ups from the sugars, fats, or oils.

helpful hints for grilling

1. Preheat the grill for at least ten minutes or until the inside temperature reaches 500–550°F.
2. Brush the hot grill to clean it.
3. Keep the cover closed so that the heat circulates evenly and the grill can impart some of the smoky flavor into the food.
4. Trim visible fat so that there is less fat to drip into the flames causing flare-ups. Keep a spray bottle of water nearby to spritz any flare-ups.
5. Oil the food, not the grill. The oil will be in the marinade or lightly rubbed on the food.
6. Use tongs to turn your food to avoid piercing the meat and having juices drip into the flames or coals, which causes flare-ups.

7. Grill presentation side first. Cook food long enough to release itself from the cooking surface to ensure visual appeal.

8. Turn food only once! Wait for caramelization (browning) before turning. This means that you don't pry it off the grill. When it is ready, you will be able to turn it easily, leaving nothing behind.

9. When is it done? Use an instant-read meat thermometer and check food frequently to ensure proper sanitation and avoid any bacteria buildup. The minimum internal temperatures should be:

   POULTRY—ground 165°F, breasts 170°F, and whole birds 180°F

   MEAT (BEEF, LAMB, PORK, VEAL)—ground 160°F, roasts 145°F,
   > Rare: 125–130°F
   > Medium rare: 130–140°F
   > Medium: 140–160°F
   > Medium well: 150–155°F
   > Well done: 160°F and above

10. Let meat rest before slicing so that the juices do not rush out when the meat is cut or sliced.

11. If you use a gas grill, keep a full spare tank on hand to avoid running out of gas while you are sitting on your deck or patio enjoying your lovely backyard surroundings.

12. The natural sugars in fresh fruits make it a great candidate for grilling. Simply cut up your favorite fruits, place on skewers, and grill until beautifully browned for a light dessert or side dish.

13. Fresh flowers from your garden such as nasturtiums and pansies, which are edible and also fresh herbs, make lovely garnishes for your special summer dishes. Be creative!

recipes

Before beginning any cooking process, you should read the recipe thoroughly before beginning so that you do not encounter any surprises! There are also some variables to consider such as wind, outside temperature, the size and shape of your ingredients, and the grill that you are using. Thinking about the particular circumstances can make a huge difference when grilling. It can also give better results. High-sugar sauces or marinades should be drained from the meat before placing on the grill to avoid flare-ups. They can be lightly brushed on the meat after it has been turned once.

grilled vegetables

This vegetable platter makes a lovely centerpiece for a buffet table. Consider your grill when slicing vegetables and cut them so that they will not fall through the grate. Varying the vegetable types and sizes will add to the appearance of your platter. Serve this with just about any dish in the book.

---

1 large eggplant, unpeeled and sliced into 1/4-inch thick rounds

1/2 teaspoon fine sea salt

2 medium zucchini, unpeeled and sliced lengthwise into 1/4-inch thick rounds

2 sweet onions, peeled and sliced into very thin rounds

1 red bell pepper, cored and sliced into 1/4-inch rounds

1 green bell pepper, cored and sliced into 1/4-inch rounds

1 yellow bell pepper, cored and sliced into 1/4-inch rounds

2 tablespoons extra virgin olive oil

1/2 teaspoon freshly ground black pepper

Fresh basil for garnish

1 | Preheat grill or grill pan.

2 | Place eggplant in bowl large enough to eventually hold all veggies. Lightly salt eggplant and let sit for 10 minutes. Add remaining vegetables and toss with olive oil. Place on preheated grill and cook to desired doneness. Season with salt and pepper as soon as vegetables are done.

3 | Garnish with fresh basil sprigs.

Chef's Secret

Some vegetables only require grilling on one side. Heat kills vitamins and minerals, so the crisper the better. Salting the eggplant draws out moisture and forms a moisture barrier to prevent the absorption of too much oil. This recipe can be made early in the day and served at room temperature. Leftovers can be used for sandwiches or tossed with pasta.

EXCHANGES/CHOICES
3 Vegetable
1/2 Fat

CALORIES 100 | CALORIES FROM FAT 35
TOTAL FAT 4.0 g | SATURATED FAT 0.5 g | TRANS FAT 0.0 g
CHOLESTEROL 0 mg | SODIUM 150 mg | POTASSIUM 410 mg
TOTAL CARBOHYDRATE 16 g | DIETARY FIBER 4 g | SUGARS 8 g
PROTEIN 2 g | PHOSPHORUS 60 mg

basic grilled chicken

SERVES: 1 | SERVING SIZE: 1 PIECE OF CHICKEN

Mastering basic grilled chicken is a very handy tool. From this, you can prepare as many dishes as you can think of. For starters, you can top a green salad, turn it into chicken salad, fill a panini, and much more. You can be as creative as your imagination will allow.

---

1 boneless, skinless chicken breast
(about 4 ounces)

1/8 teaspoon fine sea salt

1/8 teaspoon freshly ground pepper

1 | Pound chicken breast to even thickness. (This allows for more even cooking.) Season both sides with salt and pepper.

2 | Preheat grill or grill pan. Grill 3–4 minutes on each side. Do not turn the chicken until it allows you to turn it. If it sticks, it is not ready to be turned.

Chef's Secret

In order to avoid the chicken sticking to the grill or grill pan, make sure it is preheated for at least 10 minutes.

EXCHANGES/CHOICES
3 Protein, lean

CALORIES 125 | **CALORIES FROM FAT** 20
TOTAL FAT 2.5 g | **SATURATED FAT** 0.8 g | **TRANS FAT** 0.0 g
CHOLESTEROL 65 mg | **SODIUM** 330 mg | **POTASSIUM** 200 mg
TOTAL CARBOHYDRATE 0 g | **DIETARY FIBER** 0 g | **SUGARS** 0 g
PROTEIN 24 g | **PHOSPHORUS** 175 mg

sensational chicken burgers

SERVES: 4 | SERVING SIZE: 1 BURGER

I created these burgers for a neighborhood picnic. I wanted to make sure that I was going to bring something healthy as well as tasty.

1/2 pound ground chicken breast

1/2 pound ground chicken (mixed light and dark)

1/4 cup chopped sun-dried tomatoes (not in oil)

1/4 cup chopped onion

1/4 cup chopped fresh basil

1/4 cup chopped fresh flat Italian parsley

4 cloves garlic, minced

1/2 teaspoon fine sea salt

1/2 teaspoon freshly cracked black pepper

1 | Mix all ingredients together and form 4 patties. Grill 3–4 minutes on each side and serve with Guacamole (page 42).

EXCHANGES/CHOICES
1 Vegetable
3 Protein, lean

CALORIES 165 | **CALORIES FROM FAT** 55
TOTAL FAT 6.0 g | **SATURATED FAT** 1.7 g | **TRANS FAT** 0.0 g
CHOLESTEROL 80 mg | **SODIUM** 400 mg | **POTASSIUM** 550 mg
TOTAL CARBOHYDRATE 4 g | **DIETARY FIBER** 1 g | **SUGARS** 2 g
PROTEIN 24 g | **PHOSPHORUS** 215 mg

key lime swordfish with apple radish salad

SERVES: 4 | SERVING SIZE: 4 OUNCES FISH AND 1 1/4 CUP SALAD

This versatile dish can be made just as the recipe reads or you can use any fish that you like to grill. I enjoy this with tuna as well as the swordfish.

---

1 pound swordfish steak, cut into
  4 portions

2 teaspoons key lime pepper blend

APPLE RADISH SALAD

1 Granny Smith apple, diced
  (about 1 1/2 cups)

3 stalks celery, thinly sliced
  (about 1 cup)

1 tablespoon extra virgin olive oil

1/2 cup chopped fresh cilantro or
  flat Italian parsley, plus additional
  for garnish

2 limes, juiced

1 (6-ounce) bag radishes, sliced
  (about 1 1/2 cups)

2 tablespoons canned, diced
  green chilies

1/4 teaspoon fine sea salt

1/4 teaspoon freshly ground
  black pepper

1 | Sprinkle swordfish with key lime pepper blend. Heat grill pan on high heat. Add swordfish and grill first side about 4 minutes. Turn and cook second side another 4 minutes.

2 | While swordfish is cooking, prepare Apple Radish Salad. Mix all ingredients together and set aside.

3 | Place a piece of swordfish on plate with 1 cup Apple Radish Salad. Garnish with fresh cilantro sprigs.

EXCHANGES/CHOICES
1/2 Fruit
1 Vegetable
3 Protein, lean
1/2 Fat

CALORIES 215 | CALORIES FROM FAT 70
TOTAL FAT 8.0 g | SATURATED FAT 1.8 g | TRANS FAT 0.0 g
CHOLESTEROL 45 mg | SODIUM 305 mg | POTASSIUM 630 mg
TOTAL CARBOHYDRATE 13 g | DIETARY FIBER 3 g | SUGARS 7 g
PROTEIN 23 g | PHOSPHORUS 330 mg

mediterranean skirt steak

SERVES: 4 | SERVING SIZE: 4 OUNCES

Skirt steak is a very lean cut of beef that is found on the inside of the ribs. It is very thin and cooks very quickly and is great when cooked on a grill pan. When cooking beef you can assume that there will be about 30% shrinkage during cooking.

1.3 pounds skirt steak

1 tablespoon extra virgin olive oil

1/2 cup panko breadcrumbs

1 tablespoon Stress Free Cooking
Italian Seasoning Blend (page 9)

1 | Coat the steak with the olive oil. Mix panko and Stress Free Cooking Italian Seasoning Blend. Coat steak with seasoning.

2 | Grill 3 minutes on first side. Turn and grill second side until steak is medium. This will vary based on the thickness of the skirt steak. Feel it and compare it to the fleshy part of your hand between your thumb and forefinger. This is medium rare.

3 | Slice across the grain and serve with one of the salads included in this book.

EXCHANGES/CHOICES
1/2 Starch
4 Protein, lean
2 Fat

CALORIES 305 | CALORIES FROM FAT 155
TOTAL FAT 17.0 g | SATURATED FAT 5.0 g | TRANS FAT 0.5 g
CHOLESTEROL 95 mg | SODIUM 345 mg | POTASSIUM 335 mg
TOTAL CARBOHYDRATE 7 g | DIETARY FIBER 0 g | SUGARS 1 g
PROTEIN 32 g | PHOSPHORUS 190 mg

part 7
IN THE SLOW COOKER

I love using my slow cooker, especially on busy days when I am not able to be at home cooking. It is always a pleasure to be able to come home to the wonderful savory smells of dinner cooking.

To get maximum flavor from your slow cooker, you want to begin your dishes as if you were cooking on top of the stove or in the oven. It is well worth the time and effort to brown your ingredients first before putting them in the slow cooker. If all you do is place the ingredients in the crockpot you miss out on these enhanced flavors. I have heard people complain that their slow cooker dishes lack flavor and that is why. If your slow cooker does not have a liner that is capable of stovetop cooking you can use another pan and transfer the food to the crockpot after browning and deglazing. Deglaze the pan by adding water, wine, or stock to the pan while it is hot and pour this liquid and the fond (browned bits) into the crockpot.

Most recipes that require long cooking can be transferred to the crockpot. The advantage of this is that crockpots and slow cookers don't need to be tended to so you can go on and do other things. I use mine for soups, stews, sauces, including marinara, and roasts such as pork loin.

The rule of thumb for slow cookers is that most recipes will cook in 4 hours on high and 8 hours on low. Some slow cookers have timers and keep-warm features. Some also have removable liners that allow you to do the browning on top of the stove and then place the liner in the warming unit. Some also have locking lids that allow you to transport your crockpot or slow cooker easily. I have actually brought mine full of meatballs to a party on a boat because the crockpot keeps food warm for a long time without being plugged in.

RECIPES

brisket with red wine reduction

SERVES: 8 | SERVING SIZE: 4 OUNCES

This dish can be made a day or two ahead or early in the day. If you make it the day before and refrigerate it, you can skim off almost all of the fat. I think it tastes better when made a day ahead, plus there is very little work to do at serving time.

2 tablespoons extra virgin olive oil

1 beef brisket (about 3 pounds)

3 large cloves garlic, chopped

1 large onion, chopped

1 teaspoon fine sea salt

1 teaspoon coarse ground black pepper

1 1/2–2 cups dry red wine, such as Pinot Noir, Chianti, or Syrah, or beef broth, or a combination of wine and broth

1–2 tablespoons Wondra flour

Variations

You can add some sliced mushrooms to the sauce when reducing. If you'd like to make this a one-pot meal, add some potatoes, carrots, and celery to the pan before placing in the oven or slow cooker.

1 | Preheat oven to 275°F.

2 | Place enough extra virgin olive oil in the bottom of the braising or sauté pan to cover the bottom. Heat to medium high and add brisket. Cook until the brisket is nicely browned. Brown second side. While second side is browning, place garlic and onions in pan around brisket. Sprinkle salt and pepper over brisket and rub it in.

3 | You can also add some fresh herbs if you have them. A sprig of rosemary is nice.

4 | Once onions begin to brown, add wine or beef broth. It will deglaze pan and lift all the good stuff off the bottom of the pan. Transfer to a slow cooker and cook four hours on high or eight hours on low. Or, if you don't have a slow cooker, cover and place in preheated oven for 2–3 hours until fork tender. If possible, cool in the same pan. Once cooled, remove brisket to cutting board. Bring the pan juices to a boil and reduce until thickened. You can also add a sprinkle or two of Wondra flour to help thicken. Pour the sauce over the brisket and reheat covered, if desired.

EXCHANGES/CHOICES
4 Protein, lean
1 1/2 Fat

CALORIES 265 | **CALORIES FROM FAT** 115
TOTAL FAT 13.0 g | **SATURATED FAT** 4.1 g | **TRANS FAT** 0.0 g
CHOLESTEROL 90 mg | **SODIUM** 340 mg | **POTASSIUM** 340 mg
TOTAL CARBOHYDRATE 4 g | **DIETARY FIBER** 1 g | **SUGARS** 1 g
PROTEIN 30 g | **PHOSPHORUS** 250 mg

crockpot veal shoulder roast

SERVES: 8 | SERVING SIZE: 5 OUNCES OF MEAT, 3 OUNCES POTATOES

2 veal shoulder roasts (approximately
  2 pounds each)

1 cup chopped fresh parsley

1/2 cup chopped fresh basil

3/4 teaspoon fine sea salt

1 teaspoon freshly ground black pepper

1 tablespoon extra virgin olive oil

1 pint fresh cherry tomatoes

10 ounces fresh cremini mushrooms

1 cup diced onion (about 1 medium)

3 cloves garlic, minced

2 envelopes concentrated beef broth

1 cup water

1 bag Dutch baby potatoes (24 ounces)

1 | Open up the veal shoulder roasts and lay flat. Sprinkle with the parsley, basil, salt, and pepper. Reroll and tie to hold together.

2 | Place the olive oil in large sauté pan and sear the veal on all sides until nicely browned, about 3–5 minutes.

3 | Remove and place in crockpot. Add tomatoes, mushrooms, onion, and garlic to sauté pan. Cook until onions begin to brown slightly. Remove and place in crockpot. Add the beef broth and water. Stir well. Add potatoes.

4 | Cover and cook for 4 hours on high or 8 hours on low.

EXCHANGES/CHOICES
1 Starch
1 Vegetable
7 Protein, lean

CALORIES 415 | CALORIES FROM FAT 110
TOTAL FAT 12.0 g | SATURATED FAT 3.1 g | TRANS FAT 0.5 g
CHOLESTEROL 180 mg | SODIUM 560 mg | POTASSIUM 1175 mg
TOTAL CARBOHYDRATE 23 g | DIETARY FIBER 3 g | SUGARS 3 g
PROTEIN 52 g | PHOSPHORUS 490 mg

one-dish veal chop in savory gravy

SERVES: 4 | SERVING SIZE: 1/4 RECIPE

1 shoulder veal chop, with bone
(about 1 1/2 pounds)

2 teaspoons Stress Free Cooking
Seasoning Blend (page 9)

2 tablespoons extra virgin olive oil

8 ounces carrots, scrubbed and cut
into 3-inch lengths

1 large onion, coarsely chopped
(about 1 pound)

2 cloves garlic, minced

8 ounces fingerling or baby Yukon gold
potatoes

10 ounces cremini mushrooms,
cut in half (if large)

1 cup dry red wine, such as
Sangiovese or Chianti

1/2 cup fresh parsley, chopped

1/2 cup fresh basil, chopped

1 cup low-sodium chicken or veal stock

1 | Sprinkle veal chop with the Stress Free Cooking Seasoning Blend evenly on both sides.

2 | Place olive oil in large sauté pan and heat to medium. Add veal chop and cook until golden brown on each side. Remove veal chop to a plate and set aside. Place carrots, onion, garlic, potatoes, and mushrooms in pan. Cook until onion begins to brown. Add wine, parsley, basil, and chicken or veal stock. Bring to boil.

3 | Move all ingredients and veal chop to a slow cooker for 4 hours on high or 8 hours on low. If desired, sauce can be thickened by adding 1 tablespoon Wondra flour before serving. Bring sauce back to boil and cook until thickened.

EXCHANGES/CHOICES
1 Starch
3 Vegetable
3 Protein, lean
1 1/2 Fat

CALORIES 355 | CALORIES FROM FAT 100
TOTAL FAT 11.0 g | SATURATED FAT 2.1 g | TRANS FAT 0.0 g
CHOLESTEROL 110 mg | SODIUM 360 mg | POTASSIUM 1245 mg
TOTAL CARBOHYDRATE 31 g | DIETARY FIBER 5 g | SUGARS 9 g
PROTEIN 31 g | PHOSPHORUS 375 mg

cornish hens coq au vin style

SERVES: 4 | SERVING SIZE: 1/2 CORNISH HENS

I love Cornish hens because they are small and it's easy to control portion size.

2 ounces diced pancetta

1 teaspoon extra virgin olive oil

2 Cornish hens (about 3 pounds total)

2 teaspoons Stress Free Cooking Seasoning Blend (page 9)

2 cloves garlic, minced

1 cup peeled whole small onions, preferably cippoline

4 ounces carrots, diagonally cut into 1-inch pieces

10 ounces cremini mushrooms

1 cup small potatoes, such as Dutch baby, Yukon gold, or fingerling

1 1/2 cups dry red wine such as Burgundy, Merlot, or Cabernet Sauvignon

1 1/2 cups good-quality low-sodium chicken stock

1 | Place pancetta in large sauté pan with oil and cook until crispy.

2 | Cut Cornish hens in half. Sprinkle each half with Stress Free Cooking Seasoning Blend.

3 | Remove pancetta from pan and add Cornish hens, skin side down. Cook until skin is golden brown. Turn. Add garlic to pan surface. Cook until garlic becomes fragrant. Add onions, carrots, mushrooms, and potatoes. Cook 2–3 minutes. Add wine and chicken stock. Bring to a boil. Transfer everything over to a slow cooker and cook on high for 4 hours or 8 hours on low. Remove skin before serving.

Chef's Secret

Instead of finishing this dish in a slow cooker, you can also finish it in the oven. After you bring to a boil, lower heat to simmer, cover, and place covered dish in a preheated conventional oven at 400°F or convection oven at 375°F for one hour.

EXCHANGES/CHOICES
1/2 Starch
2 Vegetable
5 Protein, lean
1/2 Fat

CALORIES 350 | CALORIES FROM FAT 110
TOTAL FAT 12.0 g | SATURATED FAT 3.2 g | TRANS FAT 0.5 g
CHOLESTEROL 165 mg | SODIUM 525 mg | POTASSIUM 1120 mg
TOTAL CARBOHYDRATE 17 g | DIETARY FIBER 2 g | SUGARS 4 g
PROTEIN 40 g | PHOSPHORUS 420 mg

part 8
FINISHING TOUCHES & DESSERTS

dylan's blueberry muffins

SERVES: 12 | SERVING SIZE: 1 MUFFIN

I created this recipe for my nephew who was on a NO FAT diet. He really loved them!

---

1 cup Splenda

4 egg whites

1 teaspoon vanilla extract

12 ounces plain, nonfat yogurt

2 cups all-purpose flour

1 tablespoon baking powder

1 cup blueberries

1 tablespoon flour (to coat blueberries)

Nonstick cooking spray

1 | Preheat oven to 350°F.

2 | In a large bowl, combine Splenda, egg whites, and vanilla. Mix completely. Add yogurt.

3 | Combine flour and baking powder. Slowly add to above, until well blended.

4 | Coat blueberries lightly with flour. Add blueberries to mixture and mix well.

5 | Coat cupcake pan with nonstick pan coating. Fill cupcake pans to top with batter.

6 | Bake for 30 minutes until tops are golden or until toothpick comes out clean.

EXCHANGES/CHOICES
1 1/2 Carbohydrate

CALORIES 115 | CALORIES FROM FAT 0
TOTAL FAT 0.0 g | SATURATED FAT 0.1 g | TRANS FAT 0.0 g
CHOLESTEROL 0 mg | SODIUM 130 mg | POTASSIUM 115 mg
TOTAL CARBOHYDRATE 22 g | DIETARY FIBER 1 g | SUGARS 5 g
PROTEIN 5 g | PHOSPHORUS 185 mg

how to
MAKE MUFFINS

3   Blend until moistened.

6   Place pan liners in muffin tin.

1   Place wet ingredients in large bowl. Add vanilla.

4   Add blueberries that have been tossed with flour. This will keep them from sinking to the bottom of the bowl.

7   Using an ice cream scoop, fill the pan liners.

2   Add dry ingredients.

5   Mix well.

8   Bake as directed in the recipe (page 140).

olive oil cake with raspberries and cream

SERVES: 16 | SERVING SIZE: 1 SLICE

1/2 cup Splenda brown sugar blend

1/2 cup extra virgin olive oil

1 egg, lightly beaten

4 egg whites

1/3 cup skim milk

1 teaspoon pure vanilla extract

2 cups all-purpose flour

1 tablespoon baking powder

1/2 teaspoon fine sea salt

Nonstick pan coating

2 cups low-fat ricotta cheese

2 tablespoons Grand Marnier or raspberry liqueur

2 pints fresh raspberries

Fresh mint for garnish (optional)

1 | Preheat oven to 350°F.

2 | In a large bowl, mix brown sugar and olive oil. Add the egg and egg whites and mix completely. Add milk and vanilla. Mix well.

3 | Combine flour, baking powder, and salt. Slowly add to above, until well blended.

4 | Lightly spray cake pan. Pour into 10-inch springform pan. Smooth to an even surface.

5 | Bake 25–30 minutes or until toothpick comes out clean.

6 | Remove cake from oven. Cool slightly and cut a thin layer from the top so that you expose the nooks and crannies of the cake.

7 | Mix ricotta with liqueur. Spread ricotta over cake. Top with raspberries and chill for several hours so that ricotta blends with cake. Serve with fresh mint garnish.

Chef's Secret

Pan sizes vary, so test carefully by inserting a toothpick into the center of the cake and adjust baking time accordingly. If the toothpick comes out clean, the cake is done.

EXCHANGES/CHOICES
1 1/2 Carbohydrate
1 Protein, lean

CALORIES 200 | **CALORIES FROM FAT** 80
TOTAL FAT 9.0 g | **SATURATED FAT** 1.8 g | **TRANS FAT** 0.0 g
CHOLESTEROL 20 mg | **SODIUM** 205 mg | **POTASSIUM** 135 mg
TOTAL CARBOHYDRATE 24 g | **DIETARY FIBER** 3 g | **SUGARS** 6 g
PROTEIN 6 g | **PHOSPHORUS** 180 mg

MAKE DESSERTS HEALTHIER

Not all desserts have to be off limits. Here are some ways to make desserts a little healthier so that they fit into your healthy lifestyle.

- Use phyllo dough instead of preparing a higher-fat butter or shortening-based piecrust.

- Substitute healthy fats such as extra virgin olive oil for butter and/or shortening.

- Use equivalent applesauce, canned pumpkin, or sweet potato puree as a substitute for butter and shortening.

- Use mashed banana for half the fat of shortening.

- Incorporate more grain and fiber such as polenta or oatmeal into your desserts.

- Use the highest-quality ingredients you can afford so that you can get maximum flavor and still be satisfied with a smaller portion.

- Make individual portion-controlled desserts.

- Use egg whites instead of whole eggs. When substituting, 2 egg whites = 1 whole egg.

- Use low-fat dairy products.

- Make fruit the basis for dessert and garnish with a little something special.

- You can usually reduce the sugar in a recipe. If the recipe calls for 1 cup, try reducing the sugar to 3/4 cup or use a natural sugar substitute.

- Substitute some of the white flour in your recipes with whole-wheat flour for more fiber.

lemon chiffon with fresh berries

SERVES: 6 | SERVING SIZE: 1/2 CUP

This deliciously sweet tart dessert is very refreshing with a melt-in-your-mouth quality. It is light enough to enjoy without feeling guilty. Including fruit in a dessert helps to reduce the calorie and fat content. You can make it a day or two before a party and it will be even better once the flavors have blended.

1/3 cup fresh lemon juice, strained of seeds, about 2 large lemons

1/2 cup granulated Splenda

4 large eggs

3 cups fresh berries, such as strawberries, blueberries, and blackberries

---

Chef's Secret

Can also be layered in a large trifle dish. Lemon chiffon also makes a very nice dip for a fruit platter but you should make sure that you serve it in a bowl over some ice to keep it chilled. Granola can be added for a little crunch.

1 | Place lemon juice and Splenda in saucepan. Heat and stir until sugar dissolves. Remove from heat.

2 | Crack eggs into the bowl and whisk well. Slowly pour the lemon sugar mix into the eggs while whisking. Whisk for 1 minute, then return the egg mixture to the saucepan. Whisk and cook on low to medium for several minutes until the egg mixture thickens. (The more you whisk, the lighter the mixture will be.) This will take 2–5 minutes depending on your equipment. The mixture is ready to be removed from heat when it coats the back of a spoon. Refrigerate for one hour or more. It will thicken more as it cools.

3 | Place some of the lemon chiffon in a dessert glass or bowl and spoon berries over or layer lemon cream and berries. Top with berries.

EXCHANGES/CHOICES
1/2 Fruit
1 Protein, lean

CALORIES 90 | CALORIES FROM FAT 30
TOTAL FAT 3.5 g | SATURATED FAT 1.1 g | TRANS FAT 0.0 g
CHOLESTEROL 125 mg | SODIUM 50 mg | POTASSIUM 155 mg
TOTAL CARBOHYDRATE 11 g | DIETARY FIBER 2 g | SUGARS 7 g
PROTEIN 5 g | PHOSPHORUS 80 mg

LEMON CHIFFON WITH FRESH BERRIES

how to
MAKE A PHYLLO PIE CRUST

1   Defrost phyllo and separate the leaves.

3   Roll several leaves of phyllo and cut crosswise to make lattice crust. Toss the strips of phyllo so that they are light and airy.

5   Top with phyllo strands. Turn (pinch) the edges of the bottom crust in so that you have a nice finished edge.

2   Place leaves in pie plate. Carefully separate leaves as you work. Place additional leaves in pie plate and spray with non-stick cooking spray between each leaf.

4   Place the mixed berries in the phyllo crust.

6   Bake as directed (page 147).

mixed berry pie with phyllo crust

SERVES: 8 | SERVING SIZE: 1 PIECE

One of the ways that we can cut fat and calories from desserts is to use fruit as a main ingredient and also phyllo dough instead of butter-laden crusts.

10 sheets 9 × 14-inch frozen phyllo dough

Nonstick cooking spray

1 quart fresh strawberries, washed and cut into pieces the size of the raspberries

2 cups fresh blueberries

1 pint fresh raspberries

Chef's Secret

Phyllo should not be defrosted in the microwave or it will become too moist and gummy. When working with phyllo, it is important to keep it covered so that it does not dry out. Cover with plastic wrap and a damp towel to prevent it from becoming too dry.

1 | Defrost phyllo dough in refrigerator for 3 hours or overnight.

2 | Preheat oven to 425°. Divide phyllo in half. One half will be the bottom crust and the remaining half will be for the top crust.

3 | Spray a 9-inch pie plate with nonstick cooking spray. Place a leaf of phyllo in the pie plate and spray it. Top with another sheet of phyllo and spray. Repeat this procedure with the first half of the phyllo.

4 | Mix all the berries together and place in pie plate.

5 | Cut the remaining phyllo into 1-inch strips and toss together. Place on top of fruit. Spray with nonstick cooking spray.

6 | Place in preheated oven and bake for 20–25 minutes until crust is golden. If your crust gets too brown before 20 minutes, you can cover it with a sheet of aluminum foil.

EXCHANGES/CHOICES
1/2 Starch
1 Fruit

CALORIES 105 | **CALORIES FROM FAT** 20
TOTAL FAT 2.0 g | **SATURATED FAT** 0.3 g | **TRANS FAT** 0.0 g
CHOLESTEROL 0 mg | **SODIUM** 70 mg | **POTASSIUM** 195 mg
TOTAL CARBOHYDRATE 22 g | **DIETARY FIBER** 5 g | **SUGARS** 9 g
PROTEIN 2 g | **PHOSPHORUS** 40 mg

vanilla bean polenta with dried cherries

SERVES: 8 | SERVING SIZE: 1/2 CUP

My favorite desserts are those that are guilt-free. Having a dessert that is based on healthy ingredients such as milk and cornmeal, along with some fruit, makes it easy to do!

2 cups water

1 teaspoon of your favorite cordial,
   such as Grand Marnier or Amaretto

1 cup dried cherries

4 cups skim milk

Pinch of sea salt

1 teaspoon vanilla extract

1 cup finely ground cornmeal

1/4 cup Splenda

1 | Bring water to boil. Add liqueur and cherries and steep until cherries are soft and rehydrated.

2 | Combine milk, salt, vanilla, and Splenda in a large heavy saucepan. Bring to boil and reduce to simmer. Slowly add cornmeal. Stir constantly and cook approximately 5–7 minutes.

3 | Remove pan from heat. Allow to sit for 5 minutes. Top with cherries.

EXCHANGES/CHOICES
1 Starch
1 Fruit
1/2 Milk, fat-free

CALORIES 175 | CALORIES FROM FAT 0
TOTAL FAT 0.0 g | SATURATED FAT 0.1 g | TRANS FAT 0.0 g
CHOLESTEROL 0 mg | SODIUM 75 mg | POTASSIUM 270 mg
TOTAL CARBOHYDRATE 37 g | DIETARY FIBER 2 g | SUGARS 20 g
PROTEIN 5 g | PHOSPHORUS 250 mg

INDEX

alphabetical index

Note: Page numbers followed by *ph* refer to photographs.

a

arctic char poached with white wine, lemon, and rosemary, 76

b

baby kale salad with red onion, chick peas, and black olives, 48

baked scallops with mushroom sauce, 113

balsamic glaze for drizzling, 56

balsamic salmon on a bed of barley pilaf with tomato and basil, 81

basic grilled chicken, 127

basic vinaigrette, 37

black bean and peach salsa, 39

brisket with red wine reduction, 134

broiled flounder with tropical pineapple slaw, 114

c

cauliflower soup with prosciutto crisps and blue cheese sprinkle, 68ph, 69

chicken, pasta, and veggie bake, 112

chicken and vegetables en papillote, 108, 109ph

chicken cacciatore, 87

chicken caesar meatballs, 117

Cornish hens coq au vin style, 137

crock pot veal shoulder roast, 135

crunchy quinoa stuffed zucchini, 98ph, 99

d

Dylan's blueberry muffins, 140

e

eggplant caviar, 94

eggplant meatballs, 115

f

farro soup with mushrooms and kale, 70

fava with lemon and garlic, 66

fennel, red onion and orange salad, 50

fresh pasta, 33

fresh tomato and basil sauce, 44

g

garlic scape pesto, 41

gnudi, 22, 23ph

grilled vegetables, 126

guacamole, 42

subject index

Note: Page numbers followed by *ph* refer to photographs.

Z

zucchini

Metric Equivalents

Liquid Measurements	Metric equivalent
1 teaspoon	5 mL
1 tablespoon *or* 1/2 fluid ounce	15 mL
1 fluid ounce *or* 1/8 cup	30 mL
1/4 cup *or* 2 fluid ounces	60 mL
1/3 cup	80 mL
1/2 cup *or* 4 fluid ounces	120 mL
2/3 cup	160 mL
3/4 cup *or* 6 fluid ounces	180 mL
1 cup *or* 8 fluid ounces *or* 1/2 pint	240 mL
1 1/2 cups *or* 12 fluid ounces	350 mL
2 cups *or* 1 pint *or* 16 fluid ounces	475 mL
3 cups *or* 1 1/2 pints	700 mL
4 cups *or* 2 pints *or* 1 quart	950 mL
4 quarts *or* 1 gallon	3.8 L

Weight Measurements	Metric equivalent
1 ounce	28 g
4 ounces *or* 1/4 pound	113 g
1/3 pound	150 g
8 ounces *or* 1/2 pound	230 g
2/3 pound	300 g
12 ounces *or* 3/4 pound	340 g
1 pound *or* 16 ounces	450 g
2 pounds	900 g

Dry Measurements	Metric equivalent
1 teaspoon	5 g
1 tablespoon	14 g
1/4 cup	57 g
1/2 cup	113 g
3/4 cup	168 g
1 cup	224 g

Length	Metric equivalent
1/8 inch	3 mm
1/4 inch	6 mm
1/2 inch	13 mm
3/4 inch	19 mm
1 inch	2.5 cm
2 inches	5 cm

Farenheit	Celsius
275ºF	140ºC
300ºF	150ºC
325ºF	165ºC
350ºF	180ºC
375ºF	190ºC

Farenheit	Celsius
400ºF	200ºC
425ºF	220ºC
450ºF	230ºC
475ºF	240ºC
500ºF	260ºC

Weights of common ingredients in grams

Ingredient	1 cup	3/4 cup	2/3 cup	1/2 cup	1/3 cup	1/4 cup	2 Tbsp
Flour, all-purpose (wheat)	120 g	90 g	80 g	60 g	40 g	30 g	15 g
Flour, well-sifted, all-purpose (wheat)	110 g	80 g	70 g	55 g	35 g	27 g	13 g
Sugar, granulated cane	200 g	150 g	130 g	100 g	65 g	50 g	25 g
Confectioner's sugar (cane)	100 g	75 g	70 g	50 g	35 g	25 g	13 g
Brown sugar, packed firmly	180 g	135 g	120 g	90 g	60 g	45 g	23 g
Cornmeal	160 g	120 g	100 g	80 g	50 g	40 g	20 g
Cornstarch	120 g	90 g	80 g	60 g	40 g	30 g	15 g
Rice, uncooked	190 g	140 g	125 g	95 g	65 g	48 g	24 g
Macaroni, uncooked	140 g	100 g	90 g	70 g	45 g	35 g	17 g
Couscous, uncooked	180 g	135 g	120 g	90 g	6 0 g	45 g	22 g
Oats, uncooked, quick	90 g	65 g	60 g	45 g	30 g	22 g	11 g
Table salt	300 g	230 g	200 g	150 g	100 g	75 g	40 g
Butter	240 g	180 g	160 g	120 g	80 g	60 g	30 g
Vegetable shortening	190 g	140 g	125 g	95 g	65 g	48 g	24 g
Chopped fruits and vegetables	150 g	110 g	100 g	75 g	50 g	40 g	20 g
Nuts, chopped	150 g	110 g	100 g	75 g	50 g	40 g	20 g
Nuts, ground	120 g	90 g	80 g	60 g	40 g	30 g	15 g
Bread crumbs, fresh, loosely packed	60 g	45 g	40 g	30 g	20 g	15 g	8 g
Bread crumbs, dry	150 g	110 g	100 g	75 g	50 g	40 g	20 g
Parmesan cheese, grated	90 g	65 g	60 g	45 g	30 g	22 g	11 g